THE KORAN

THE KORAN

AN EDITION PREPARED FOR ENGLISH
READERS · BEING AN ARRANGEMENT
IN CHRONOLOGICAL ORDER FROM THE
TRANSLATIONS OF EDWARD W. LANE,
STANLEY LANE-POOLE & A. H. G. SARWAR

ILLUSTRATED BY VERA BOCK

AVENEL BOOKS · NEW YORK

ISBN: 0-517-138964

Library of Congress Catalog Card Number: 74-78429
This edition is published by Avenel Books
a division of Crown Publishers, Inc.
by arrangement with P. P. Press
b c d e f g h
Manufactured in the United States of America

A NOTE ON MOHAMMED AND THE KORAN

BEFORE *Mohammed, the religion of the Arabs was a kind of fetish-ism, with many gods — sun, stars and moon, as well as lesser fetishes like mountains, trees and stones. The Jewish and Christian religions were well known but not adopted, although many inquiring minds were seeking a monotheistic worship; and there was a widespread belief in the coming of a prophet with such a revelation. A group of* hanifs *denied the fetishes and asserted the existence of a single divinity; but they failed to formulate a ritual or a doctrine, and it remained for Mohammed to establish, single-handed, the religion which is still all-dominant in the Arab world.*

He was born in 570 or 571, and came from the powerful tribe of the Koriesh, guardians of the Kaaba, the temple of the idols at Mecca. His particular branch of the tribe was poor, and he became a shepherd; but in his twenties he married a rich wife, and had the status of a prosperous merchant. He subscribed to the religion of the time, outwardly at least, until the age of forty, when he heard a voice which ordered him to cry out the truth of a one supreme deity. At first he thought he was possessed by devils, but the voice claimed to be the angel Gabriel, and told Mohammed he was to be the mes-senger of God. So he began to preach, and further revelations came. In this first period his speeches were mystical and poetic.

After three years of inspired preaching in Mecca, he had only a dozen or two converts. By the fifth year he was preaching not only for one God, but against the idolatry of many gods, and his speeches threatened all unbelievers with hell-fire. At this point his tribe of the Koriesh began to persecute his followers; for the Koriesh guarded the idols, and collected the pilgrims' tolls, and they could not tolerate this doctrine. Mohammed himself was protected by blood-relation-ship to many tribal chiefs. His continued fiery preaching, despite all hindrances, and his manly bearing under difficulties, gradually earned him a following made up of influential leaders, chiefs, and swordsmen. This group performed its rites publicly at the Kaaba, in view of the whole city, until the Koriesh took sterner measures, out-lawing Mohammed's whole clan. Gradually his followers slipped away from Mecca to Medina, where a colony of Jews had laid the groundwork for a belief in one God; and in 622, eluding the Koriesh, he fled to Medina also. This is the hejira or flight of Mohammed, from which Islam dates its history.

In Medina, Mohammed became a king, and his speeches became those of a lawgiver. But his dominance was threatened from within and without. He suppressed, exiled, and killed the rebels, and then turned to fight the Koriesh, who could not tolerate Medina's control of the caravan route taken by pilgrims to Mecca. The Koriesh were defeated in 626, and made a truce with Mohammed. But when they broke this truce, his followers swept upon Mecca, captured the city, and destroyed in one day the 360 idols of the Kaaba. Mohammed pardoned his defeated enemies, and his hold over the Arab world became complete.

The Koran is the official compilation of the preachings of the Prophet. Since his message was essentially the same for years on end, the Koran is a book of repetition upon repetition. It is, moreover, an even more confusing book than mere repetition can make it. It is arranged by chapters or suras not in chronological or ideological order, but mechanically by length of sura, with the longest first and the shortest last. This is an almost complete reversal of the original order, for the first preachings were short poetic revelations, while the last preachings were long dogmatic ones.

German scholarship in the last century established the original order of the suras, and for the general reader such chronological order gives the Koran far more coherence. But the general reader needs even more editing than this, to eliminate some of the multiplicity of repetition. Two English scholars, Edward William Lane and Stanley Lane-Poole, therefore made separate versions for the general reader. Lane made his selections on the basis of subject matter, Lane-Poole on the basis of chronological order.

In the present version we have made use of the entire Lane-Poole version, and most of the Lane version. In addition we have taken additional chapters and parts of chapters from the recent translation of A. H. G. Sarwar. At the end of each passage we give the number of the sura and the initial of the translator: L for Lane, P for Lane-Poole, and S for Sarwar. The first sura given is a rewriting from other sources.

The chapter titles are those of the original; except that when bracketed one of two things is indicated: Either the chapter is not reprinted complete, or selections have been taken from a number of chapters dealing with the same subject. Except for the compilations of Bible stories and mythology, the chapters are generally in the original order of their delivery by the Prophet.

THE KORAN

THE CONTENTS OF THIS EDITION

THE KORAN OF MOHAMMED

THE POETIC PERIOD

A. D. 609-613

PRAISE be to God, the Lord of the Worlds!
The Compassionate, the Merciful!
King of the day of judgment!
Thee we worship, and Thee we ask for help.
Guide us in the straight way,
The way of those to whom Thou art gracious;
Not of those upon whom is Thy wrath, nor of the erring.

ONE WHO IS MANTLED

IN THE NAME OF GOD,
THE COMPASSIONATE, THE MERCIFUL

ARISE, O Thou Mantled One; Arise and warn, and magnify thy Lord!

Go and purify thy garments, and fly from every abomination. Bestow not your favors in hopes of greater returns, but persevere for the sake of your Lord. Then when the trumpet is sounded, that day shall be a severe day for the unbelievers, anything but easy!

Let me alone with him whom I have made, to whom I have given vast riches, and sons before his eyes; on whom I have made great bestowals, and who covets I should add still more. Never! Surely he is a denier of our signs! I will cause him to carry a great load to a great height, because he thought and he weighed; then he denied! Again he denied. How he weighed! and again he denied! O how he weighed, then looked about, then frowned and scowled, then deliberated, and swelled with pride, and said: "This is nothing but an enchantment which has been learned from others; this is nothing but the words of a man." I will throw him into the flames of hell.

What shall make you understand the flames of hell? They burn up a man completely; they leave nought and spare nought. Over this conflagration are nineteen angels appointed, angels who are holy messengers; and We have given you their numbering only to throw discord among those who disbelieve, and that those who have been given the Book may be convinced, and the believers may increase their faith, and the faithful may not doubt; and that those whose hearts are diseased, and the unbelievers, may say: "What does God intend by naming this number?" Thus does God cause to err whomever He pleases, and directs aright whomever He pleases. For no one knows the hosts of the Lord except Himself, and this is nothing else but a reminder to mankind.

Most surely! By the moon, and the night when it retreats, and the dawn when it reddens, the fire of hell is a most grievous thing, a terrible warning to men. Each soul will be given to it as a payment for what it has done — excepting the companions of the right hand: they shall be dwelling in green gardens, asking one another questions about the wicked, and saying to the guilty themselves: "What brought you into the conflagration?" And they will answer: "We were not among those who prayed, and we were not among those who fed the poor; we argued in idle disputes, and we denied the Day of Judgment, until death overtook us"; and then the pleading of friends can do no good.

What aileth them, then, that they turn from the reminding of the Book like timid asses running from the roaring of a lion? Nay, every man of them desires that he may be given open sheets of revelation from God! Never! And they fear not the Time to come. Never again: this is sufficient warning; whoso wishes to be warned, is warned; but he will not be warned, unless God please. He is worthy of reverence, and He is generous in bestowing pardon. [lxxiv]

THE BACKBITER

WOE to every backbiter, slanderer! Who hath heaped up riches and counted them over! He thinketh that his riches have made him everlasting: nay! he shall surely be cast into Blasting Hell. And what shall teach thee what Blasting Hell is? The fire of God kindled, reaching over the hearts; verily it is over him like a tent, with stays well-stretched. [civ, P]

SUPPORT

WHAT thinkest thou of him who calleth the Day of Judgment a lie? He it is who driveth away the orphan, and is not urgent

for the feeding of the poor. Woe then to those who pray, those who are careless in their prayers, who make a pretence, but withhold support. [cvii, P]

12 THE NIGHT

By the Night when she spreadeth her veil, by the Day when it is manifested, by what made the male and the female: verily your aims are diverse.

Then as for him who giveth alms and feareth God, and putteth his faith in the Best, we will speed him onward to ease. And as for him who is covetous and desirous of riches, and denieth the Best, we will speed him onward to trouble; and his riches shall not avail him when he falleth down into Hell. Verily ours is the guiding, and ours the latter and the former life.

And I have warned you of a flaming fire: none shall be burned in it but the wretch, who hath called it a lie and turned his back. But the righteous shall be guided away from it — he that giveth his substance in charity, and doeth no man a kindness in hope of reward, but only in seeking the face of his Lord the Most High; and in the end he shall surely be well pleased. [xcii, P]

THE COUNTRY

I swear by this country — and thou art a dweller in this country — and by father and child! Verily we have created man amid trouble: — doth he think that no one shall prevail against him? He saith "I have squandered riches in abundance": doth he think that no one seeth him? Have we not made him two eyes, and a tongue and two lips, and pointed him out the two highways? Yet he doth not attempt the steep one. And what shall teach thee what the steep one is? The ransoming of captives, or feeding on the day of famine the orphan of thy kindred or the poor that lieth in the dust;

finally, to be of those who believe, and enjoin steadfastness on each other, and enjoin mercy on each other: — these are the people of the right hand. And those who disbelieve in our signs, they are the people of the left: over them a Fire closeth. [xc, p]

THE SPLENDOR OF MORNING

By the splendor of morning, and the still of night! Thy Lord hath not forsaken thee nor hated thee; and the future will surely be better for thee than the present, and thy Lord will surely give to thee and thou wilt be well pleased. Did He not find thee an orphan and sheltered thee, and found thee erring and guided thee, and found thee poor and enriched thee? ·Then as for the orphan, oppress him not, and as for him who asketh of thee, chide him not away, and as for the bounty of thy Lord, tell of it.· [xciii, p]

THE MEASUREMENT

Surely We have sent the Koran down during the night of measurement. And what shall make thee comprehend what the night of measurement is? The night of measurement is better than a thousand months. The messenger-spirits and the great spirit Gabriel come down therein by the order of their Lord with all the commandments. There is Peace: — It lasts till the rise of the morn. [xcvii, s]

THE NIGHT-COMER

By the heaven and the night-comer. And what shall make thee comprehend what the night-comer is? It is the bright star — there is no soul but has a guardian thereon. Then let man see what he is made of. He is made out of liquid poured forth. Coming out from between the backbone and the breastbone. Most sure He is capable of causing him to return. The

13

day all secrets shall be exposed, and he shall have neither might nor helper. By the heaven which comes back, and the earth which splits asunder, most surely this Koran is a decisive word, and it is no joke. Surely they plot a plot, and I plot a plot; therefore give time to the unbelievers; give them time for a little while. [lxxxvi, s]

THE SUN

By the sun and his noonday brightness, and the moon when she follows him, and the day when it shows his splendor, and the night when it covers him, by the heaven and Him who built it, by the earth and Him who leveled it, by the soul and Him who perfected it, then He taught it the ways of its ruin and the way of its safety. Surely he succeeds who purifies it; and surely ruined is he who corrupts it. Thamud in their transgression belied the truth. When the worst wretched man amongst them rose up, then the messenger of God told them about the she-camel of God and her watering. But they treated him as a liar and hamstrung her. Then their Lord overthrew them on account of their sin and He leveled them all, nor was He afraid of the consequences. [xci, s]

HE FROWNED

He frowned and turned aside, because the blind man came to him. And what shall make thee comprehend — that perhaps he wanted to purify himself, or that he would mind and then his minding would do him good. But as to him who was independent, then thou wast after him, though thou wast not responsible for his purification. But as to him who came to thee striving, and he stood in awe of God, then thou didst show negligence towards him. No, no! surely these verses are a reminder, then let him who wishes, mind it, written on honored sheets, exalted, purified, with the hands of scribes honorable and virtuous. Disapproved be man! what makes him choose disbelief? Out of what object has he been made? Out of a life-germ! He made him, then proportioned him. Then He made his way easy for him, then He causes him to die and He causes him to be buried. Then when He pleases He will cause him to rise up. Nay, he has not carried out what He commanded him to do. Therefore let man examine his food: because We poured down the water a great pouring, and then We split the earth a splitting so that We cause to grow therein grain, and grapes and herbs, and olives and dates, and orchards with dense trees, and fruits and pasture, an enjoyment for you and your cattle. Then when the roaring blast comes — that day will man fly from his brother, and his mother and his father, and his female companion and his sons. For every man that day there shall be an affair which will sufficiently occupy him. Some faces that day shall be bright, laughing, happy. And other faces that day shall have dust upon them, darkness shall cover them: they are the unbelievers and the wicked.   [lxxx, s]

THE MOST HIGH

MAGNIFY the name of thy Lord, The Most High, who created, and fashioned, and decreed, and guided, who bringeth forth the pasturage, then turneth it dry and brown.

We will make thee cry aloud, and thou shalt not forget, except what God pleaseth; verily He knoweth the plain, and the hidden. And we will speed thee to ease. Admonish, therefore, — verily admonishing profiteth, — whoso feareth God will mind; and there will turn away from it only the wretch who shall broil upon the mighty fire; and then shall neither die therein, nor live. Happy is he who purifieth himself, and remembereth the name of his Lord, and prayeth, but ye prefer the life of this world, though the life to come is better and more enduring. Truly this is in the books of eld, the books of Abraham and Moses.   [lxxxvii, P]

THE FIG

By the fig and the olive, by mount Sinai, by this territory inviolate, surely We have made man in the best of proportions, then We throw him back to the lowest of the low; but as to those who believe and do good deeds, for them, then, is a reward never to be cut off; what, then, after this causes thee (O man!) to belie the judgment? Is not God of all judges the Best?   [xcv, s]

THE CLUSTERS OF STARS

By the heaven, full of clusters of stars, and by the promised day, and by the witness and one for whom the evidence is given, disapproved be the companions of the trenches of fire, possessors of fuel, when they sit down thereupon; and they see what they do to the believers. And they were not enraged against them except because they believed in God, all-Mighty, all-Praised — He to whom belongs the kingdom of the heavens and the earth. And God sees everything. Surely as to those who persecute believing men and believing women and then turn not to God, for them then is the agony of hell, and for them is the burning agony. Surely as to those who believe and do good deeds, for them are gardens beneath which flow rivers. This is the great triumph. Most surely the seizing of thy Lord is severe. Surely He starts creation and He causes it to return. And He is all-Forgiving, all-Loving. Master of the glorious Power, absolute Doer of what He desires. Hast the news of the hosts come to thee of Pharaoh and Thamud? Nay, those who choose disbelief belie the truth. And God surrounds them on all sides. Nay, it is a glorious Koran well guarded in a tablet.   [lxxxv, s]

THE WRAPPED UP

O THOU wrapped up! Wake the night except a little — half of it, or make it a little less than that, or make it a little more, and recite the Koran evenly with clear recitation. Surely We are going to lay a weighty word upon thee. Surely the getting up at night is the strongest way to conquer one's self and the most upright in respect of pronunciation. Surely thou hast a long occupation during the day. Therefore remember the name of thy Lord at night and devote thyself towards Him with a complete devotion. Lord of the east and the west, there is no deity but He, therefore take him as a Protector. And be persevering in spite of what they say and leave them alone a noble leaving, and let Me deal with those who declare the truth to be a lie, who are possessors of plenty, and give them a little time. Surely We have ready fetters and a pit of fire. And a choking food and a painful agony. The day when the earth shall shake and the mountains also, and the mountains shall become heaps of flowing sand. Surely We have sent towards you a messenger, being a witness over you, as We sent a messenger towards Pharaoh. Then Pharaoh disobeyed the messenger, therefore We seized him a most calamitous seizing; therefore how will you save yourselves, if you disbelieve, on the day which will turn children into grey-haired persons? The day in which the sky shall clear up, his promise must be fulfilled. Surely this is a reminder, therefore let him who pleases take a way unto his Lord.

Surely thy Lord knows that thou wakest the night nearly two-thirds thereof, and half thereof, and one-third thereof and a party of those with thee also. And God measures the night and the day. He knows that you will not be able to keep it up, therefore He turns towards you with mercy; hence recite the Koran, what is easy thereof. He knows that there will be some amongst you who are sick and others moving in the earth seeking God's grace and still others fighting in God's path; therefore recite whatever is easy thereof, but keep up the prayers and pay the stated alms and offer to God a goodly offering. And whatever good you send forward for your souls you will find it with God what is better and larger

in reward. And ask God's forgiveness. Surely God is Forgiving, Merciful. [lxxiii, s]

THE SMITING

THE Smiting! what is the Smiting? And what shall teach thee what the Smiting is? The Day when men shall be like scattered moths, and the mountains like carded wool! Then as for him whose scales are heavy — his shall be a life well-pleasing. And as for him whose scales are light — his abode shall be the Bottomless Pit. And what shall teach thee what that is? A Raging Fire! [ci, P]

THE QUAKING

WHEN the earth shall quake with her quaking, and when the earth hath cast forth her burdens, and man shall say, "What aileth her?" on that day shall she tell out her tidings, because thy Lord doth inspire her. On that day shall men come in companies to behold their works, and whosoever hath wrought an ant's weight of good shall behold it, and whosoever hath wrought an ant's weight of evil shall behold it. [xcix, P]

THE RENDING ASUNDER

WHEN the Heaven is rent asunder, and when the stars are scattered, and when the seas are let loose, and when the tombs are turned upside-down, the soul shall know what it hath done and left undone. O man! what hath deceived thee respecting thy Lord, the Generous; who created thee, and fashioned thee, and moulded thee aright? In what form it pleased him He builded thee. Nay! but ye take the Judgment for a lie! But verily there are watchers over you — worthy reporters — knowing what ye do. Verily the righteous shall be in delight, and the wicked in Hell-Fire: they shall be burnt at it on the day of doom, and they shall not be hidden from it. What shall teach thee what is the Day of Judgment? Again, what shall teach thee what is the Day of Judgment? A day when no soul can avail aught for another soul, for the ordering on that day is with God. [lxxxii, P]

THE WRAPPING

WHEN the sun shall be wrapped up, and when the stars shall fall down, and when the mountains shall be removed, and when the ten-month camels shall be neglected, and when the wild beasts shall be huddled together, and when the seas shall boil over, and when souls shall be joined to their bodies, and when the child that was buried alive shall be asked for what crime she was slain; and when the Books shall be laid open, and when the sky shall be peeled off, and when Hell shall be set a-blaze, and when Paradise shall be brought near, — the soul shall know what it hath wrought.

And I swear by the stars that hide, that move swiftly and hide, and by the darkening night, and by the breath of dawn, — verily this is the word of a noble messenger, strong, firm in the favor of the Lord of the Throne, obeyed and trusted. And your companion is not mad: of a surety he saw the Angel on the clear horizon: and he is not mistrusted as to the unseen, nor is his the speech of a pelted devil. Then whither go ye? Verily this is but a Reminder to the worlds, to whomsoever of you chooseth to walk aright: but ye shall not choose it, except God choose it, the Lord of the worlds. [lxxxi, P]

THE RENDING ASUNDER

WHEN the sky is rent asunder, and when it listens to its Lord and it is right that it should do so, and when the earth is spread larger, and throws out what is therein and becomes hollow, and it listens to its Lord and it is right that it should do so — O man! surely thou hast to labor and labor towards thy Lord, then thou shalt meet him. Then as to one who

is given his book in his right hand, his reckoning shall be made an easy one, and he will return to his family joyfully. But as to him who is given his book behind his back, then he will call for death. And he shall enter the flaming fire. Surely he used to be joyful in his family. Surely he believed that he would never reappear. Yea! surely His Lord was seeing him. Then no! I call to witness the sunset redness, by the night and what moves on therein, and by the moon when it is full. You shall most surely have to ascend state after state. Then what is the matter with them that they believe not? And when the Koran is recited to them they bow not down. Nay! those who choose disbelief belie the truth. And God knows best what they conceal in their hearts. Therefore give them the news of a painful agony. But as to those who believe and do good deeds for them is a reward not to be cut off. [lxxxiv, s]

THE CHARGERS

By the Chargers that pant, and the hoofs that strike fire, and the scourers at dawn, who stir up the dust with it, and cleave through a host with it!

Verily Man is thankless towards his Lord, and verily he is witness thereof, and verily in his love of weal he is grasping. Doth he not know? — when what is in the tombs shall be laid open, and what is in men's breasts shall be laid bare; verily on that day their Lord shall know them well! [c, p]

THE NEWS

Of what do they question together? Of the great News, about which they dispute? Nay, but they shall know! Again, — Nay, but they shall know! Have we not made the earth as a bed? and the mountains as tent-pegs? and created you in pairs, and made your sleep for rest, and made the night for a mantle, and made the day for bread-winning, and built above you seven firmaments, and put therein a burning lamp, and sent down water pouring from the squeezed clouds to bring forth grain and herbs, and gardens thick with trees?

Lo! the Day of Decision is appointed — the day when there shall be a blowing of the trumpet, and ye shall come in troops, and the heavens shall be opened, and be full of gates, and the mountains shall be removed, and turn into mist. Verily Hell lieth in wait, the goal for rebels, to abide therein for ages; they shall not taste therein coolness nor drink, save scalding water and running sores, — a meet reward! Verily they did not expect the reckoning, and they denied our signs with lies; but everything have we recorded in a book: — "Taste then: for we will only add torment to you." Verily for the pious is a place of joy, gardens and vineyards, and full-bosomed girls, their mates, and a cup brimming over: there shall they hear neither folly nor lying; — a reward of thy Lord — a gift sufficient, of the Lord of the heavens and of the earth, and of what is between them, the Merciful! They shall not obtain speech of him: — on the day when the Spirit and the Angels shall stand in ranks, they shall have no utterance, save he to whom the Merciful shall give leave, and who speaketh rightly.

That is the day of truth! Then he that chooseth, let him make for his Lord as his goal. Verily we warn you of torment nigh at hand; on the day when men shall see what his hands have sent before him, and the unbeliever shall say, "Oh! that I were dust." [lxxviii, P]

THE OVERSHADOWING EVENT

Has the news of the overshadowing event come to thee? Some faces on that day shall be cast down. They shall be laboring, toiling, entering into hot fire. They shall be made to drink of a boiling spring. They shall have no food but a dry thorn bush. It neither fattens nor satisfies hunger. And other faces

on that day shall be pleased, well satisfied with their strivings, residing in a high garden. Thou shalt hear no vain talk therein, therein are flowing springs, therein are raised thrones, and goblets ready placed, and carpets laid out in rows. And mattresses of velvet spread out. Do they not then examine the clouds how they are made? and the heaven how it is made high? and the mountains how they are erected? and the earth how it is spread out? Therefore go on reminding. Thou art but a reminder, thou art not a superintendent over them. But as to him who turns back and disbelieves, then God will cause him to suffer the great suffering. Surely towards Us is their coming back, then surely it is for Us to take their account. [lxxxviii, s]

THE DAYBREAK

By the daybreak, and the ten nights, and the even and the odd, and the night when it moves on, is there not in these things an oath and a matter for evidence, for one possessed of understanding? Hast thou not seen how thy Lord did with 'Ad and the people of Aram possessors of lofty columns, such as have not been made in any other cities? and Thamud who hewed out huge rocks in the valley? and Pharaoh the lord of hosts? Those who transgressed in the cities and they did get evil therein. Therefore thy Lord let down upon them a kind of suffering. Most surely thy Lord is watching, and as for man when his Lord disciplines him so that He honors him and blesses him; then he says: "My Lord has honored me." But when He disciplines him so that He measures out his provision, then he says: "My Lord has degraded me." Nay, but you do not honor the orphan, nor do you urge the feeding of the poor, and you squander the property left by the deceased persons a great squandering. And you love wealth with a whole-hearted love. Nay, when the earth is leveled out with beating after beating, and thy Lord manifests Himself, and the messenger-spirits come, row after row; and when He will bring forth hell, that day man will begin to mind, and whence can minding come to him then? He will say: "O would that I had sent forward for my living here." But on that day no one causes to suffer as He does, and no one binds as He binds. "O soul made tranquil! Come back to thy Lord satisfying and satisfied. Therefore enter thou amongst My servants, and enter thou in My garden." [lxxxix, s]

[THE RESURRECTION, PARADISE AND HELL]

WHEN one blast shall be blown on the trumpet, and the earth shall be raised and the mountains, and be broken to dust with one breaking, on that day the Calamity shall come to pass: and the heaven shall cleave asunder, being frail on that day, and the angels on the sides thereof; and over them on that day eight of the angels shall bear the throne of thy Lord. On that day ye shall be presented for the reckoning; none of your secrets shall be hidden. And as to him who shall have his book given to him in his right hand, he shall say, "Take ye, read my book; verily I was sure I should come to my reckoning." And his shall be a pleasant life in a lofty garden, whose clusters shall be near at hand. "Eat ye and drink with benefit on account of that which ye paid beforehand in the past days."

But as to him who shall have his book given to him in his left hand, he shall say, "O would that I had not had my book given to me, nor known what was my reckoning! O would that my death had been the ending of me! My wealth hath not profited me! My power is passed away from me!" "Take him and chain him, then cast him into hell to be burnt, then in a chain of seventy cubits bind him: for he believed not in God, the Great, nor urged to feed the poor; therefore he shall not have here this day a friend, nor any food save filth which none but the sinners shall eat." [lxix, L]

23

THE FACT

WHEN the Fact becomes fact, none shall deny it is a fact, — abasing, — exalting! When the earth shall be shaken in a shock, and the mountains shall be powdered in powder, and become like flying dust, and ye shall be three kinds.

Then the people of the right hand — what people of good omen! And the people of the left hand — what people of ill omen! And the outstrippers, still outstripping: — these are the nearest to God, in gardens of delight; a crowd of the men of yore, and a few of the latter days; upon inwrought couches, reclining thereon face to face. Youths ever young shall go unto them round about with goblets and ewers and a cup of flowing wine, — their heads shall not ache with it, neither shall they be confused; and fruits of their choice, and flesh of birds to their desire; and damsels with bright eyes like hidden pearls, — a reward for what they have wrought. They shall hear no folly therein, nor any sin, but only the greeting, "Peace! peace!"

And the people of the right hand — what people of good omen! Amid thornless lote-trees, and bananas laden with fruit, and shade outspread, and water flowing, and fruit abundant, never failing, nor forbidden, and wives exalted — verily we produced them specially and made them virgins, amorous, of equal age, for the people of the right hand, — a crowd of the men of yore, and a crowd of the latter days.

But the people of the left hand — what people of ill omen! — Amid burning wind and scalding water, and a shade of black smoke, not cool or grateful! Verily, before that, they were prosperous; but they persisted in the most grievous sin, and used to say, "When we have died, and become dust and bones, shall we indeed be raised again, and our fathers the men of yore?" Say: Verily those of yore and of the latter days shall surely be gathered to the trysting-place of a day which is known. Then ye, O ye who err and call it a lie, shall surely eat of the tree of Zakkum, and fill your bellies with it, and drink upon it scalding water, — drink like the thirsty camel: — this shall be their entertainment on the Day of Judgment!

It is we who created you; why then will ye not believe? Have ye considered the germs of life — is it ye who create them, or are we the creators? It is we who have decreed death among you; yet are we not debarred from changing you for your likes, or producing you how ye know not. But ye have known the first creation: why will ye not mind? Have ye considered what ye sow? Is it ye who raise it, or are we the raisers thereof? If we pleased we could surely make it dry, so that ye would stop and marvel, saying "We have spent, yet we are forbidden the fruits." Have ye considered the water ye drink? Is it ye who send it down from the clouds, or do we send it down? If we pleased we could make it salt; why will ye not be thankful? Have ye considered the fire which ye kindle? Is it ye who make the wood that produces it, or do we make it? It is we who have made it for a reminder and a benefit to the traveler. Then magnify the name of thy Lord the Most Great.

And I swear by the setting-places of the stars, and that, if ye knew it, is verily a mighty oath, verily this is the honorable Koran, written in the preserved Book: let none touch it but the purified; — a revelation from the Lord of the worlds. Will ye then disdain this discourse, and make it your daily bread to discredit it? Why then when the dying man's soul has come up to his throat, and ye at the moment are watching — and we are nearer to him than ye, although ye see us not, — why, if ye are to have no Judgment, do ye not cause that soul to return, if ye speak the truth? But if he be one of those brought nearest to God, there is rest for him and sweet odor and a garden of delights. And if he be of the people of the right hand, he shall be greeted with "Peace to thee," from the people of the right. And if he be of those who call it

a lie, the erring, then an entertainment of scalding water, and broiling in Hell. Verily this is assured truth! So magnify the name of thy Lord the Most Great. [lvi, P]

26 THE ASCENTS

A QUESTIONER questioned about the agony which is to befall the unbelievers; there is no one to prevent its coming from God, Master of the ascents. The messenger-spirits and the great spirit ascend towards Him during a day the measure of which is fifty thousand years. Therefore persevere thou a noble persevering. They see it far, but We see it near. On that day when the heaven shall be like molten brass in color, and the mountains shall be like colored wool, and no warm friend shall inquire about his warm friend, they shall be put in sight of each other. The guilty person would wish to redeem himself from the agony of that day by offering his children, and his female companion and his brother and his relations who sheltered him and those who are in the earth put together — that then he might rescue himself.

Never! surely it is a burning flame, dragging away the skins, claiming him who turns back and runs away, and who gathers wealth and looks after it. Surely man is born of a fickle temperament; when evil touches him he is full of lamentations, but when good befalls him he is niggardly, excepting those who pray: those who are constant in their prayers, and those in whose wealth there is a fixed portion for the beggar and the wretched, and those who trust in the day of judgment, and those who stand in awe of the agony of their Lord — surely the agony of their Lord is not a thing to be careless of — and those who restrain their appetites except with their wives or what their right hands possess, because then they are not to be blamed; but they who seek to go beyond that, they then are the breakers of the laws, and those who are faithful of their trusts and their covenants, and those who are upright in their evidence, and those who keep guard over their prayers, they shall be in gardens, honored.

But what is the matter with those who choose disbelief, those coming running toward thee from the right hand and the left, crowds upon crowds? Does each man amongst them covet to enter the garden of bliss? Never! Surely We have made them out of what they know. But no! I swear by the Lord of the easts and the wests, most surely We are capable of replacing them by those better than themselves, and We cannot be defeated. Therefore let them indulge in idle talk and let them play till they meet their day which is held out to them. The day they shall come out of their burial places hastening as if they were being shot towards a target. Their eyes cast down, covered with disgrace: this is the day which was held out to you. [lxx, s]

THE MERCIFUL

THE merciful hath taught the Koran; he created man, taught him clear speech; the sun and the moon in their courses, and the plants and the trees do homage. And the Heaven, He raised it, and appointed the balance. (That ye should not transgress in the balance: — but weigh ye justly and stint not the balance.) And the Earth, He prepared it for living things, therein is fruit, and the palm with sheaths, and grain with its husk, and the fragrant herb: Then which of the bounties of your Lord will ye twain deny? He created man of clay like a pot, and He created the Jinn of clear fire: Then which of the bounties of your Lord will ye twain deny? Lord of the two Easts, and Lord of the two Wests: Then which of the bounties of your Lord will ye twain deny? He has let loose the two seas which meet together; yet between them is a barrier they cannot pass: Then which of the bounties of your Lord will ye twain deny? He bringeth up therefrom pearls great and small: Then which of the bounties of your Lord will ye twain deny? And His are the ships towering on the sea like mountains: Then which of the bounties of your Lord will ye twain deny? All on the earth passeth away, but the face of thy Lord abideth endued with majesty and honor: Then which of the bounties of your Lord will ye twain deny? All things in the Heaven and Earth supplicate Him, every day is He at work: Then which of the bounties of your Lord will ye twain deny? We will apply ourselves to you, O ye two notables: Then which of the bounties of your Lord will ye twain deny? O company of Jinn and men, if ye are able to compass the boundaries of the Heavens and of the Earth, then compass them; but ye shall not compass them, save in our might: Then which of the bounties of your Lord will ye twain deny? There shall be shot at you a flash of fire and molten brass; ye cannot defend yourselves: Then which of the bounties of your Lord will ye twain deny? And when the Heaven shall be rent and become rosy like a red hide: Then which of the bounties of your Lord will ye twain deny? On that day neither man nor Jinn shall be asked about their sin: Then which of the bounties of your Lord will ye twain deny? The sinners shall be known by their signs, and they shall be seized by the forelock and the feet: Then which of the bounties of your Lord will ye twain deny? "This is Hell which the sinners took for a lie," to and fro shall they wander between it and water scalding hot: Then which of the bounties of your Lord will ye twain deny? But for him who feareth the majesty of his Lord shall be two gardens: Then which of the bounties of your Lord will ye twain deny? With trees branched over: Then which of the bounties of your Lord will ye twain deny? And therein two flowing wells: Then which of the bounties of your Lord will ye twain deny? And therein of every fruit two kinds: Then which of the bounties of your Lord will ye twain deny? Reclining on couches with linings of brocade and the fruit of the gardens to their hand: Then which of the bounties of your Lord will ye twain deny? Therein the shy-eyed maidens neither man nor Jinn hath touched before: Then which of the bounties of your Lord will ye twain deny? Like rubies and pearls: Then which of the bounties of your Lord will ye twain deny? Shall the reward of good be aught but good? Then which of the bounties of your Lord will ye twain deny? And beside these shall be two other gardens: Then which of the bounties of your Lord will ye twain deny? Dark green in hue: Then which of the bounties of your Lord will ye twain deny? With gushing wells therein: Then which of the bounties of your Lord will ye twain deny? Therein fruit and palm and pomegranate: Then which of the bounties of your Lord will ye twain deny? Therein the best and comeliest maids: Then which of the bounties of your Lord will ye twain deny? Bright-eyed, kept in tents: Then which of the bounties of your Lord will ye twain deny? Man hath not touched them before, nor Jinn: Then which of the bounties of your Lord will ye twain deny? Reclining on green cushions and fine carpets: Then which of the bounties of your Lord will ye twain deny? Blessed be the name of thy Lord endued with majesty and honor.　　　　　　　　　　　　　　　[lv, P]

THE RHETORICAL PERIOD

A.D. 613-615

THE MOON

THE Hour approacheth and the moon is cleft asunder. But if they see a sign they turn aside, and say "Useless magic!" And they call it a lie, and follow their own lusts: — but everything is ordained. Yet there came to them messages of forbiddance — Wisdom supreme — but warners serve not!

Then turn from them: the Day when the Summoner shall summon to a matter of trouble, with eyes cast down shall they come forth from their graves, as if they were scattered locusts, hurrying headlong to the summoner: the unbelievers shall say, "This is a hard day!"

The people of Noah, before them, called it a lie, and they called our servant a liar, and said, "Mad!" and he was rejected. Then he besought his Lord, "Verily I am overpowered: defend me." So we opened the gates of heaven with water pouring forth, and we made the earth break out in springs, and the waters met by an order foreordained; and we carried him on a vessel of planks and nails, which sailed on beneath our eyes; — a reward for him who had been disbelieved. And we left it as a sign; but doth any one mind? And what was my torment and warning? And we have made the Koran easy for reminding; but doth anyone mind?

'Ad called it a lie; but what was my torment and warning? Lo, we sent against them a biting wind on a day of settled ill-luck. It tore men away as though they were trunks of palm-trees torn-up. But what was my torment and warning? And we have made the Koran easy for reminding; but doth any one mind?

Thamud called the warning a lie: and they said, "A single mortal from among ourselves shall we follow? verily then we should be in error and madness. Is the reminding committed to him alone among us? Nay, he is an insolent liar." They shall know tomorrow about the insolent liar! Lo! we will send the she-camel to prove them: so mark them well, and be patient. And predict to them that the water shall be divided between themselves and her, every draught taken in turn. But they called their companion, and he took and hamstrung her — And what was my torment and warning? Lo! we sent against them one shout; and they became like the dry sticks of the hurdle-maker. And we have made the Koran easy for reminding; but doth any one mind?

The people of Lot called the warning a lie; — Lo! we sent a sand-storm against them, except the family of Lot, whom we delivered at daybreak as a favor from us; thus do we reward the thankful. And he had warned them of our attack, but they misdoubted the warning; and they sought his guests, so we put out their eyes. "So taste ye my torment and warning!" And in the morning there overtook them a punishment abiding. "So taste my torment and warning." And we have made the Koran easy for reminding; but doth any one mind?

And there came a warning to the people of Pharaoh: they called our signs all a lie: so we gripped them with the grip of omnipotent might.

Are your unbelievers better men than those? Is there immunity for you in the Books? Do they say, "We are a company able to defend itself?" They shall all be routed, and turn their backs. Nay, but the Hour is their threatened time, and the Hour shall be most grievous and bitter. Verily the sinners are in error and madness! One day they shall be dragged into the fire on their faces: "Taste ye the touch of Hell."

Verily all things have we created by a decree, and our command is but one moment, like the twinkling of an eye. And we have destroyed the like of you: — but doth any one mind? And everything that they do is in the Books; everything, little and great, is written down. Verily the pious shall be amid gardens and rivers, in the seat of truth, before the King Omnipotent.   [liv, P]

33

NOAH

SURELY We sent Noah to his people saying: "Warn thy people before the painful agony overtakes them." He said: "O my people! surely I am a clear warner to you. That ye serve God and reverence Him and obey me. He will forgive you your sins and give you time till a fixed term. Surely the

term of God when it comes cannot be put off, if you knew."
He said: "My Lord! I have called my people by night and
by day, but my calling has increased them in nothing but
aversion. And surely whenever I called them that Thou
mightest forgive them, they put their fingers in their ears,
and wrapped themselves in their clothes and persisted in
denial and swelled with pride a great swelling: then surely
I called them loudly, and then I called them in public and I
spoke to them in secret a secret speech, and I told them,
'Ask forgiveness of your Lord, surely He is very forgiving,
He will send down rain upon you abundantly. And He will
strengthen you with wealth and children and He will make
for you gardens and He will make for you rivers. What is
the matter with you that you expect not great gifts from
God? And surely He has made you fashion after fashion.
Do you not see how God has made seven heavens one above
the other? and He has placed the moon as a light in them
and He has made the sun as a lamp. And God has caused
you to be grown out of earth a kind of growing vegetation.
Then He will cause you to return to it and He will bring you
another bringing forth. And God has spread out the earth
for you that you may walk therein by open way.'"

Noah said: "My Lord! surely they have disobeyed me and
followed one whose wealth and children increase him in
nothing but loss. And they have planned a great plan. And
they say: "Forsake not your deities and forsake neither Wadd
nor Swaa; neither Yaghus, nor Ya'uq, nor Nasr. And they
have surely caused a great many to be lost, and increase
not the unjust people except in error." They were drowned
on account of their sins and were made to enter fire; then
they found no one besides God as helpers. And said Noah:
"My Lord! leave not upon the land a single dwelling of the
unbelievers; surely if Thou leave them, they will cause Thy
servants to be lost and they will not give birth except to a
sinner, a great disbeliever. My Lord! forgive me and my

parents and he who joins my house being faithful, and the faithful men and the faithful women. And increase not the unjust people except in destruction. [lxxi, s]

THE TIME

DID not a long period of time pass over man when he was not anything worth mentioning? We have made man out of a life-germ (sperm) uniting with another (ovum). We are going to discipline him, so We have made him hearing, seeing. Surely We have guided him in the path, he is either grateful or ungrateful. Surely for the ungrateful We have prepared chains and shackles and a flaming fire. Surely the virtuous shall drink of a cup tempered with camphor. A spring from which the servants of God will drink, they will make it flow a great flowing. They fulfill their vows and fear the day whose calamity shall be far-reaching; and in spite of their own want, they give food to the poor, and the orphan and the prisoner, "We feed ye for the sake of God alone, we desire from you neither recompense nor thanks. Surely we fear from our Lord a day of sadness and distress." Then God will save them the evil of that day and cause them to meet with cheerfulness of face and happiness of mind. He will reward them, on account of their having persevered, with a garden and silk dress: reclining therein upon thrones, they shall not see either the sun or biting cold, and the shades of the garden shall be close upon them, and its fruits shall be within easy reach. And cups of silver and goblets of crystal shall be made to go round them, and other goblets of silver cut like crystal which they shall measure according to a measure. And they shall be given to drink a cup tempered with ginger, a spring therein called salsabeel the softly flowing. And abiding youths shall go round them whom when thou seest thou wouldst think them to be pearls scattered about. And whenever thou shalt look there, thou shalt see blissful-

35

ness and a great kingdom. Their over garments are robes made of green fine silk and of thick brocade, and they shall be given to wear bangles of silver and their Lord shall give them to drink a pure drink. "Surely this is a reward for you and your striving has been accepted."

Surely We have sent down upon thee this Koran a gradual sending down. Therefore persevere thou for the sake of the judgment of thy Lord and obey not anyone of them, any sinner or ungrateful person. And remember thou the name of thy Lord morning and evening. And during the night bow down to Him and glorify Him till late at night. Surely these people love this near life and leave behind them a grievous day. We have made them and We have strengthened their formation and whenever We please We can replace them by their likes a complete replacement. Surely this is a reminder, then whoever wishes, takes a way to his Lord. And you wish not except as God wishes; surely God is Knowing, Wise. He causes to enter, whom He pleases, in His mercy. And as to the unjust He has prepared for them a painful agony.   [lxxvi, s]

K.

K. By the glorious Koran. Nay, they marvel that a warner from among themselves hath come to them: and the unbelievers say, "This is a marvelous thing! When we are dead and are become dust! — that is a far-fetched return!" We know what the earth consumeth of them, and with us is a book that keepeth count. Nay, they called the truth a lie when it came to them, but they are in a perplexed state. Will they not look up to the heaven above them, how we built it, and beautified it, and there are no flaws therein? And we spread out the earth, and cast stable mountains upon it, and caused to grow there plants of all beauteous kinds, for consideration and warning to every repentant servant. And we sent down water from heaven as a blessing, and caused thereby gardens and harvest grain to grow, and tall palm-trees with spathes heaped up, a provision for our servants; and revived thereby a barren land. Like that shall the resurrection be. Before them the people of Noah and the people of Er-Rass and Thamud called the prophets liars, and 'Ad, and Pharaoh, and the brethren of Lot, and the people of the grove, and the people of Tubba' — one and all called the apostles liars, — and found the threat true. Were we then impotent as to the first creation? yet they are in doubt about a new creation. We created man, and know what his soul whispereth, and we are nearer to him than his jugular vein.

When the two note-takers take note, sitting on the right hand and on the left, not a word doth he utter, but a watcher is by him ready. And the stupor of death shall come in truth; — "this is what thou would'st have avoided." And the trumpet shall be blown, — that is the Day of the Threat! And every soul shall come, along with a driver and a witness — "Thou didst not heed this: so we have taken away from thee thy veil, and today thy sight is keen."

And his companion shall say, "This is what I am ready to witness." "Cast ye into Hell every unbelieving rebel, hinderer of the good, transgressor, doubter, who setteth up other gods with God; cast ye him into the fierce torment." His companion shall say, "O our Lord! I misled him not; but he was in fathomless error." God shall say, "Wrangle not before me, for I charged you before about the threat. My word does not change, and I am not unjust to my servants." On that day will we say to Hell, "Art thou full?" and it shall say, "Is there more?" And Paradise shall be brought nigh to the righteous, not afar: — "This is what ye were promised, unto every one who turneth himself to God and keepeth His laws, who feareth the Merciful in secret, and cometh with a contrite heart; enter it in peace": — that is the Day of Eternity! They shall have what they please therein, and increase at our hands.

37

And how many generations have we destroyed before them, mightier than they in valor! then seek through the land — is there any refuge? Verily in that is a warning to him who hath a heart, or giveth ear, and is a beholder. And We created the heavens, and the earth, and what is between them, in six days, and no weariness touched us. Then be patient with what they say, magnify thy Lord with praise before the rising of the sun and its setting, and in the night magnify Him, and in the endings of the prayers. And give ear to the day when the crier shall cry from a near place, the day when they shall hear the shout in truth — that is the day of resurrection! Verily it is we who give life and death, and to us do all return. The day when the earth shall gape asunder over them suddenly — that is the gathering easy to us! We know well what they say: and thou art not a tyrant over them. But warn by the Koran him who feareth the threat. [l, P]

THE ROCK

A TIME will come when those who have chosen disbelief would wish that they were Moslems. Leave them to eat and enjoy themselves a little and let their hopes wile them away. But in the future they will know. And We have not destroyed any town but that it had a term made known to it. No community can hasten on its term nor can they postpone it. And they say: "O thou upon whom has been sent down the reminder, thou art most certainly a mad man. Why dost not thou bring to us messenger-spirits if thou be of the truthful?" We do not send down the messenger-spirits except with the truth, and when that happens they are not allowed any time. We Ourselves surely send down the reminder and We most surely are its guardians. And most surely We have sent messengers before thee amongst ancient tribes. And no messenger ever came to them but they laughed at him. In this way do We cause the mocking of messengers to enter the hearts of the guilty. They will not believe in the Koran, and they have the precedent of the ancients before them. And were We to open for them an entrance in space and they were to climb therein the whole day, they would surely say: "Our eyes have been merely bewildered, rather we have been mesmerized."

And most certainly We have made clusters of stars in space and We have adorned it for the spectators. And We guard it against every evil-one driven away. But whoever wishes to listen by stealth, then he is followed by a flaming fire. And We have extended the earth, and We have put mountains therein and We have caused to grow therein everything in due proportion.

And We have made for you therein means of livelihood, and for those whom you do not feed. And there is nothing of which there are not vast treasures with Us but We send not down except in a known measure. And We send the laden winds, then We send down from above water. Then We cause you to drink it. And you are not the treasurers thereof.

And most surely We Ourselves cause life and We cause death and We Ourselves are the Heirs. And most certainly We know those of you who go forward, and most certainly We know those who lag behind. And surely thy Lord is He who will gather them together; surely He is Wise, Knowing.

And most surely We have made man out of sounding clay, out of black smelling mud. And We made the jinn before that, out of burning fire. And remember when thy Lord said to the messenger-spirits, "Surely I am going to make a human being out of sounding clay, out of black smelling mud. So that when I have formed him into a complete shape and I have breathed into him of My spirit, then start bowing down to him."

Then the messenger-spirits bowed down all of them together, but the disappointed-one did not. He did not agree to be with those who bowed down. He said: "O disappointed-

39

one! what reason hast thou not to be with those who bowed
down?" He replied: "It is not for me to bow down to a
human being whom Thou hast made out of sounding clay,
out of black smelling mud." He said: "Then get out of this
state, for thou art surely driven away. And surely upon thee
be the disapproval to the day of the judgment."

He said: "My Lord! then give me time up to the day of their
being raised up." He said: "Thou art certainly of those who
are given time, to the day of the well-known appointment."
He said: "My Lord, as Thou hast caused me to deviate, I
will surely make things fair-seeming to them in this earth,
and I will cause them to deviate altogether saving those of
them who are exclusively Thy servants." He said: "This
exclusive service is the straight path that leads to Me. Surely
as to My servants thou hast no authority over them, excepting him who out of the misguided ones follows thee. And
surely hell is the certain promised place of them all. It has
seven entrances; for each entrance there is an appointed
portion of them."

Surely those who practice reverence shall be in gardens and
springs, "Enter ye therein with Peace, safeguarded." And
We take out of their breasts all kinds of hatred, turned into
brethren, seated upon thrones facing each other. No fatigue
shall touch them therein nor shall they be driven out. Inform
thou My servants that as to Me, surely I am all-Forgiving,
all-Merciful. And also that as to Mine agony — that is a most
painful agony.   [xv, s]

Y. S.

Y. S. By the wise Koran! Verily thou art of the Messengers
upon the straight way. A revelation of the Mighty, the Merciful: — to warn a people whose fathers were not warned, and
themselves are heedless. Our word has proved true against
the most of them; yet they will not believe! Verily we have

put shackles on their necks, reaching to the chin, and their heads are tied back; and we have put a barrier before them and a barrier behind them, and we have covered them so that they see not; and it is all one to them whether thou warn them or warn them not: they will not believe. Thou wilt only warn to good purpose him who followeth the monition and feareth the Merciful in secret: so tell him good tidings of forgiveness and a noble reward. Verily it is we who quicken the dead, and write down the deeds they have sent before them and the vestiges they leave behind them; and everything do we set down in the plain Exemplar.

And frame for them a parable — the people of the town of Antioch, when the Apostles came to it; when we sent unto them two, and they called them liars; so we strengthened them with a third, and they said, "Verily we are sent unto you." The people said, "Ye are only men like us; and the Merciful hath not revealed aught; in sooth ye are only lying." They said, "Our Lord knoweth that we are indeed sent unto you; and there is naught laid upon us but to announce a plain message." The people said, "Of a truth we have drawn an evil augury from you: unless ye desist, we will surely stone you, and a painful punishment shall surely betide you from us." They said, "Your evil augury is with yourselves! If ye be warned? — Nay! ye are an ignorant people." And there came from the furthest part of the city a man running: he said, "O my people! follow the Apostles, Follow those who ask you not for recompense, and who are guided aright. And what is in me, that I should not worship Him who made me and to whom we must return? Shall I take gods beside Him? If the Merciful be pleased to afflict me, their intercession will not avail me aught, nor will they deliver me; verily in that case I should be in a manifest error. Verily I believe in your Lord: therefore hear ye me." — It was said, "Enter into Paradise," and he said, "Would that my people knew how that my Lord hath forgiven me and hath

made me one of the honored!" And afterwards we sent not down upon his people armies out of heaven nor what we were wont to send down: it was but one shout, and lo, they were extinct!

O the pity of men! No apostle cometh to them but they laugh him to scorn. Do they not consider how many generations we have destroyed before them? Verily they shall not return to them, but gathered together before us shall they all be arraigned.

And a sign for them is the dead earth which we quicken and bring thereforth grain, and they eat of it; and we make gardens of palm-trees and vines, and cause springs to gush forth therein; that they may eat of its fruits, and of the labor of their hands: and will they not be thankful? Extolled be the glory of Him who hath created all sorts of what the earth beareth, and of men's selves, and of that they know not of! And a sign for them is the night. We draw away the day from it, and lo! they are in darkness; and the sun hasteneth to her resting-place. — This is the ordinance of the Mighty, the Wise! — and for the moon we have decreed his mansions, till he is wasted to the likeness of a withered palm-branch. It is not meet that the sun should overtake the moon, nor the night outstrip the day; but each doth swim in its sphere. And it is a sign for them that we carry their off-spring in the burthened ship; and that we create for them the like of it to ride on; and if we please, we drown them, and there is no succor for them, nor are they delivered save in our mercy, and for a transient joy. And when it is said to them, "Fear what is before you and what is behind you; haply ye may obtain mercy": thou bringest not one sign of the signs of their Lord but they turn away from it! And when it is said to them, "Give alms of what God hath bestowed on you," they who disbelieve say to those who believe, "Shall we feed him whom God can feed if He pleases? verily ye are only in manifest error."

And they say "When will this threat come to pass, if ye be speakers of truth?" They await but a single blast; it shall smite them whilst they are wrangling, and they shall not be able to make their wills, and unto their families they shall not return. And the trumpet shall be blown, and behold they shall hasten out of the graves to their Lord: saying, "Oh, woe is us! who hath roused us from our sleeping-place? This is what the Merciful threatened; and the apostles spake truth." There shall be but one blast, and, lo! all are arraigned before us; and on that day no soul shall be wronged at all, nor shall ye be recompensed save for what ye have wrought. Verily on that day the people of Paradise shall be happy in their pursuits, they and their wives reclining on couches in the shade; they have fruit there and whatsoever they demand: "Peace" is their greeting from a merciful Lord.

"Separate ye this day, O ye sinners! Did I not charge you, O sons of Adam, not to serve the Devil, — surely he is your open enemy, — but to worship Me: this is the straight way? Yet he led away a great multitude of you: had ye no wits? This is Hell, which ye were threatened with: roast there today, because ye did not believe." On that day will we set a seal on their mouths, but their hands shall speak to us, and their feet shall bear witness of what they have earned for themselves. And if we pleased, we could put out their eyes, and still would they hasten on their way: but how would they see? And if we pleased we could transform them as they stand so that they could not go on or turn back; and him whom we make old, we bow down his body: have they no wits?

We have not taught Mohammed poetry, nor would it befit him. It is only a warning and a plain Koran, to warn whosoever liveth: and the sentence shall be carried out upon the unbelievers. Do they not see that we have created for them, of what our hands have made, the cattle which they possess? And we have subdued them unto them, and some of them

are for riding and of some they eat, and they have in them profit and milk to drink, and will they not be thankful? But they have taken other gods beside God, if haply they may be holpen: they are not able to help them; yet they themselves are an army arrayed for their defense.

But let not their speech grieve thee: verily, we know what they hide and what they show! Doth not man see that we created him from a germ? Yet, behold he is an open adversary, and he putteth arguments to us, and forgetteth his creation, saying, "Who can quicken bones that are rotten?"

Say: he who first made them to be shall quicken them: for all creating He knoweth well; — who made for you fire from a green tree, and behold, ye kindle with it; and is not He who created the Heavens and the Earth able to create their like? Yea! for He is the wise Creator. His command, when he willeth a thing, is only to say to it "Be," and it is!

Then extolled be the Perfection of Him in whose hand is the empire over all, and to whom we must return.   [xxxvi, P]

THE JINN

SAY: "It has been revealed to me that a party of the jinn listened." Then they said: "Surely We have heard a wonderful Koran. It guides towards righteousness and we have believed in it. And we will never join anyone whatsoever with our Lord. And that He — far high is the majesty of our Lord — has not taken a female companion nor a child, and that the foolish amongst us used to say exaggerated things against God: and that we thought that neither men nor jinn would speak a lie against God: and that some individuals amongst men used to take refuge with some individuals amongst the jinn, so they increased them in haughtiness: and that they thought just as you thought that God would not raise up anyone: and that we have felt the space above and have found it filled with strong guards and flames: and that we used to sit down in some of the sitting places to listen, but whoever now tries to listen meets with a flame lying in wait for him: and that we know not whether it is evil which is meant for those on earth or whether their Lord means right guidance: and that there are some amongst us who are good and some amongst us who are otherwise: we are divided into different sects: and that we believe that in no case can we escape GOD in this earth and that we cannot escape by flying: and that when we heard the guidance we believed in it; so that whoever believes in his Lord, then let him not be afraid of either loss or high-handedness: and that some amongst us are Moslems and some amongst us are unjust, therefore whoever is Moslem, they are then the people whose objective is righteousness: and as to the unjust, they then shall be the fuel of hell." And say thou that if they keep to the right path We will give them to drink of abundant water in order that We may test them therewith. And whoever turns away from the remembrance of his Lord He will make him join a rising agony; and that the mosques belong to God, therefore call not upon anyone with God. And that when the servant of God stood up calling upon Him, they desired to crowd over him.

Say: "I only call upon my Lord! and I join not anyone with Him." Say: "Surely I am not master of either hurt or good for you." Say: "Surely no one can rescue me from God, nor do I find any place of refuge besides Him. It is but a communication from God, and His messages." And whoever disobeys God and His messenger then surely for him there is the fire of hell abiding therein all the time. Wait until when they see what is held out to them, then they will soon know who is weaker in respect of help and smaller in numbers. Say: "I know not whether what is held out to you be near or whether my Lord will make its time long." He is the Knower of the unseen and He informs no one about His secrets except the messenger whom He chooses, and surely He causes

a guard to march in front of him and behind him. So that He may know that they have delivered the messages of their Lord, and He encompasses what they have, and He counts the number of all things. [lxxii, s]

THE KINGDOM

BLESSED be He in whose hand is the Kingdom: and He is powerful over all; who created death and life to prove you which of you is best in actions, and He is the Mighty, the Very Forgiving; who hath created seven heavens in stages: thou seest no fault in the creation of the Merciful; but lift up thine eyes again, dost thou see any cracks? Then lift up thine eyes again twice; thy sight will recoil to thee dazzled and dim. Moreover, we have decked the lower heaven with lamps, and have made them for pelting the devils, and we have prepared for them the torment of the flame.

And for those who disbelieve in their Lord, the torment of Hell: and evil the journey to it! When they shall be cast into it, they shall hark to its braying as it boileth; — it shall well-nigh burst with fury! Every time a troop is thrown into it, its keepers shall ask them, "Did not a warner come to you?" They shall say, "Yea! a warner came to us; but we took him for a liar, and said, 'God hath not sent down anything. Verily, ye are only in great error.'" And they shall say, "Had we but hearkened or understood, we had not been among the people of the flame!" And they will confess their sins: so a curse on the people of the flame! Verily they who fear their Lord in secret, for them is forgiveness — a great reward. And whether ye hide your speech, or say it aloud, verily He knoweth well the secrets of the breast! What! shall He not know, who created? and He is the subtle, the well-aware! It is He who hath made the earth smooth for you: so walk on its sides, and eat of what He hath provided — and unto Him shall be the resurrection. Are ye sure that He who is in the

Heaven will not make the earth sink with you? and behold, it shall quake! Or are ye sure that He who is in the Heaven will not send against you a sand-storm, — so shall ye know about the warning! And assuredly those who were before them called it a lie, and how was it with their denial? Or do they not look up at the birds over their heads, flapping their wings? None supporteth them but the Merciful: verily He seeth all. Who is it that will be a host for you, to defend you, if not the Merciful? verily the unbelievers are in naught but delusion! Who is it that will provide for you, if He withhold His provision? Nay, they persist in pride and running away! Is he, then, who goeth groveling on his face better guided than he who goeth upright on a straight path?

Say: it is He who produced you and made you hearing and sight and heart — little are ye thankful! Say: it is He who sowed you in the earth, and to Him shall ye be gathered. But they say, "When shall this threat me, if ye are speakers of truth?" Say: the knowledge thereof is with God alone, and I am naught but a plain warner. But when they shall see it nigh, the countenance of those who disbelieved shall be evil, — and it shall be said, "This is what ye called for." Say: Have ye considered — whether God destroy me and those with me, or whether we win mercy — still who will save the unbelievers from aching torment? Say: He is the Merciful: we believe in Him, and in Him we put our trust — and ye shall soon know which it is that is in manifest error! Say: Have ye considered if your waters should sink away tomorrow, who will bring you running water?   [lxvii, P]

THE CHILDREN OF ISRAEL

EXTOLLED be the glory of Him who conveyed his servant by night from the Sacred Mosque to the furthest mosque, whose precincts we have blessed, to show him our signs! Verily, He it is who heareth and seeth! And we gave the Book of the Law

47

to Moses and made it a guide to the Children of Israel —
"Take ye no guardian beside me, seed of those whom we
bare in the ark with Noah! Verily he was a grateful servant!"
And we ordained for the Children of Israel in the Book, —
"Ye shall surely work iniquity in the earth twice, and ye
shall be puffed up with a mighty arrogance." So when the
threat came to pass for the first of the two sins, we sent upon
you servants of ours armed with grievous punishment; and
they went among your houses, and the threat was carried
out. Then in turn we gave you victory over them, and helped
you with riches and sons, and made you a very numerous
host. If ye do well, ye will do well to your own souls, and if
ye do ill, it will be to them also. And when the threat came
to pass for the second sin, — the enemy came to afflict you,
and to enter the mosque as they entered it the first time, and
to utterly destroy what they had overpowered. Haply your
Lord will have mercy on you! and if ye turn, we will turn;
but we have made Hell for a prison for the unbelievers.

Verily this Koran guideth to the right way and giveth good tidings to believers, who do that which is right, that for them
is a great reward; and that for those who believe not in the
life to come, we have made ready an aching torment.

Man prayeth for evil as for good: for man was ever hasty.

We have made the night and the day for two signs: then we
blot out the sign of the night, and make the sign of the day
manifest, that ye may seek bounty from your Lord, and may
know the number of the years and the reckoning of time;
and we have defined everything definitely. And every man's
fate we have fastened about his neck. And we will bring to
him on the day of Resurrection a book which shall be offered
to him open: — "Read thy Book: thou thyself art accountant
enough against thyself this day." He who is guided, for his
own good only shall he be guided, and he who erreth but to
his own hurt; and one burthened soul shall not be burthened
with another's burthen.

And we did not punish until we had sent an apostle. And when we resolved to destroy a city, we enjoined its men of wealth, but they disobeyed therein; so the sentence proved true, and w destroyed it utterly. How many generations have we swept away since Noah! and thy Lord knoweth and seeth enough of the sins of His servants.

Whoso desireth the present life, we will present him with what we please therein, to whom we choose: finally, we will make Hell for him to roast in, disgraced and banished: but whoso desireth the life to come, and striveth after it strenuously, and he a believer, — the endeavor of these shall be acceptable: to all, to those and those, will we extend the gifts of thy Lord; and the gifts of thy Lord are not limited. See how we have made some of them excellent above others! but the life to come is greater in degrees and greater in excellence.

Set no other god with God, lest thou sit down disgraced and defenseless. Thy Lord hath ordained that ye worship none but Him; and kindness to your parents, whether one or both of them attain old age with thee: then say not to them, "Fie!" neither reproach them; but speak to them generous words, and droop the wing of humility to them out of compassion, and say, "Lord, have compassion on them, like as they fostered me when I was little." (Your Lord knoweth perfectly what is in your souls, whether ye be well-doers; and verily He is forgiving to the repentant.) And render to thy kinsman his due, and to the poor and to the son of the road (but lavish not wastefully; truly the wasteful are brothers of the Devil, and the Devil is ungrateful to his Lord:) but if thou turnest away from them, to seek the mercy which thou hopest from thy Lord, yet speak to them gentle words. And let not thy hand be chained to thy neck; nor yet stretch it forth right open, or thou wilt sit down in reproach and destitution. Verily thy Lord will be openhanded with provision for whom He pleaseth, or He will be sparing; He knoweth and seeth His servants. And slay not your children for fear of want:

we will provide for them. Beware! verily killing them is a great sin. And draw not near to inchastity; verily it is a foul thing, and evil is the course. And slay not the soul whom God hath forbidden you to slay, unless for a just cause: and whosoever shall be slain wrongfully, we give his heir the right of retaliation; but let him not exceed in slaying; verily he is protected. And approach not the substance of the orphan, except to make it better, till he cometh to maturity: and observe your covenants; verily covenants shall be acquired of hereafter. And give full measure when ye measure, weigh with an even balance; that is best and fairest in the end. And follow not that of which thou hast no knowledge: the hearing, the sight, and the heart, — all of them shall be inquired of. And walk not proudly on the earth: verily thou shalt never cleave the earth, nor reach to the mountains in height! All that is evil in thy Lord's eye, an abomination.

That is part of the wisdom which thy Lord hath revealed to thee. And make no other god beside God, or thou wilt be thrown into Hell in reproach and banishment. Hath then the Lord assigned to you sons, and shall He take for himself daughters from among the angels? verily ye do say a tremendous saying! And we made variations in this Koran to warn them; yet it only increaseth their repulsion. Say: If there were other gods with Him, as ye say, they would then seek occasion against the Lord of the throne. Extolled be His glory, and be He greatly exalted far above what they say! The seven heavens, and the earth, and all that is therein, magnify Him, and there is naught but magnifieth his praise; only ye understand not their worship. Verily He is forbearing, forgiving. When thou declaimest the Koran, we put between thee and those who believe not in the life to come a close veil; and we put coverings over their hearts, lest they should understand it, and deafness in their ears. And when thou tellest of thy Lord in the Koran as One, they turn their backs in repulsion. We know well what they listen for, when they listen to thee, and when they whisper apart, when the wicked say, "Ye do but follow a man enchanted." See what comparisons they make for thee! but they wander and cannot find the way.

They say, "What! when we have become bones and dust, shall we forsooth be raised as a new creature?" Say: Yes! were ye stones, or iron, or any creature, the hardest to raise again that your minds can imagine. But they will say, "Who shall restore us?" Say: He who began you in the beginning! And they will wag their heads at thee and say, "When shall this be?" Say: Maybe it is nigh at hand. — A day when God shall summon you and ye shall answer with His praise; and ye shall think that ye have tarried but a little while. And say to my servants that they speak pleasantly: verily the Devil provoketh strife among them; verily the Devil is man's open enemy. Your Lord knoweth you well; if He please He will have mercy on you; or if He please He will torment you; and we have not sent thee to be our governor over them! Thy Lord knoweth well who is in the heavens and in the earth. And we distinguished some of the prophets above others, and we gave to David the Psalms. Say: Call ye upon those whom ye profess beside Him; but they will have no power to put away trouble from you or alter it. Those whom they invoke do themselves strive for access to their Lord, which of them shall be nearest: and they hope for His mercy and fear His torment: verily the torment of thy Lord is to be dreaded. There is no city but we will destroy it before the Day of Resurrection, or torment it with grievous torment. That is written in the Book.

Nothing hindered our sending thee with signs but that the people of yore called them lies. We gave Thamud the she-camel before their very eyes, but they maltreated her; and we send not a prophet with signs except to terrify. And when we said to thee, "Verily thy Lord encompasseth mankind"; — and we made the vision which we showed thee, and the

accursed tree in the Koran, only to prove men; and we will terrify them; but it shall only add to their great disobedience. And when we said to the angels, "Bow down to Adam": and they all bowed down save Iblis: who said, "What! shall I bow down to him whom thou hast created of clay?" And said, "Dost thou consider this one whom thou hast honored above me? Verily, if thou didst spare me till the day of Resurrection, I would utterly destroy his offspring, all but a few!" God said, "Begone; but whosoever of them followeth thee, verily, Hell is to be your reward — reward enough! And tempt whom thou canst of them by thy voice; and assail them with thy horsemen and thy footmen, and share with them in their riches and their children, and make them promises. (But the Devil's promises are deceitful.) Verily thou hast no power over my servants: and thy Lord sufficeth for a defender."

It is your Lord who driveth your ships on the sea, that ye may seek of His abundance, verily He is merciful to you. And when a harm befalleth you at sea, they whom ye call on beside Him are missing! Then when He bringeth you safe to land, ye stand aloof: for man was ever thankless. Are ye sure that He will not swallow you up on the shore, or send a sandstorm against you? then ye would not find for you any defender. Or are ye sure that He will not turn you back again to sea, and send against you a storm of wind and drown you, because ye were thankless? Then shall ye find for your selves no helper against us. And we have honored the sons of Adam; and we have borne them on the land and on the sea, and have fed them with good things, and distinguished them above many of our creatures.

On a day we will summon all men with their scripture: then whoso is given his book into his right hand, — these shall read their book and not be wronged a whit. And he who has been blind in this life shall be blind in the life to come, and miss the road yet more.

And verily they had well-nigh tempted thee from what we revealed to thee, to forge against us something false; and then they would have taken thee to friend; and had we not prevented thee, thou hadst well-nigh inclined to them a little: in that case we would have made thee to taste a torment double in life and double in death, then shouldst thou find for thyself no helper against us. And they well-nigh frightened thee from the land, to drive thee out of it; but if they had, they should only have tarried a little while behind thee. This was our custom with our apostles whom we sent before thee, and thou shalt find no changing in our custom.

Perform prayer from the setting of the sun till the fall of night, and the recital at dawn, — verily the recital at dawn is witnessed: and watch thou part of the night as a voluntary service; it may be that thy Lord will raise thee to a place of praise: and say: O my Lord, cause me to enter with a right entry, and to come forth with a right forthcoming, and grant me from thyself a power of defense. And say: Truth is come and falsehood is fled: verily falsehood is a fleeting thing.

And we send down from the Koran healing and mercy to the faithful; but it shall only add to the ruin of the wicked. And when we are gracious to man, he turneth away and standeth aloof; but when evil touches him he is in despair. Say: Every one doeth after his own fashion, but your Lord knoweth perfectly who is best guided on the road. And they will ask thee of the Spirit; Say: The Spirit cometh at my Lord's behest, and ye are given but scant knowledge. And assuredly, if we pleased we could take away what we have revealed to thee: then wouldst thou not find for thyself a defender against us, save in mercy from thy Lord; verily His bounty towards thee is great. Say: Surely if mankind and the Jinn united in order to produce the like of this Koran, they could not produce its like, though they helped one another. We have varied every kind of parable for men in this Koran, but most men consent only to discredit it.

55

56

And they say, "We will by no means believe in thee till thou makest a spring to gush forth for us from the earth; or till there cometh to thee a garden of palm-trees and grapes, and thou makest rivers to gush forth abundantly in its midst; or thou make the heaven to fall down in pieces upon us, as thou pretendest; or bring God and the angels before us; or thou have a house of gold; or thou ascend up into Heaven; and we will not believe in thy ascent until thou send down to us a book which we may read." Say: Extolled be the glory of my Lord! Am I aught save a man, a messenger? And nothing prevented men from believing, when the guidance came to them, but their saying, "Hath God sent a mere man as a messenger?" Say: Had there been angels upon the earth walking at ease, we had surely sent them an angel from heaven as an apostle. Say: God is witness enough between me and you: verily He knoweth and seeth His servants. And whom God guideth, he is guided, and whom He misleadeth, thou shalt find him no protectors beside Him; and we will gather them on the day of Resurrection upon their faces, blind, and dumb, and deaf, hell is their abode; so oft as its fire dieth down, we will stir up the flame. This is their reward, for that they believed not our signs, and said, "When we are become bones and dust, shall we indeed be raised a new creature?" Do they not see that God, who created the heavens and the earth, is able to create their likes? and He hath made an appointed term for them: there is no doubt of it; but the wicked consent only to deny it! Say: If ye possessed the treasures of the mercy of thy Lord, ye would then assuredly keep them, in fear of spending: for man is niggardly.

Heretofore We brought to Moses nine evident signs: Ask then the Children of Israel the story — when he came unto them, and Pharaoh said unto him, "Verily I consider thee to be bewitched, O Moses." He said, "Thou knowest that none hath sent these down as proofs but the Lord of the heavens and the earth; and verily I consider thee, O Pharaoh, accursed." So he sought to drive them out of the land; but we drowned him and those with him, every one. And after this we said to the Children of Israel, "Dwell ye in the land, and when the promise of the life to come befalleth, we will bring you in a troop to judgment." And in truth have we sent down the Koran, and in truth came it down, and we have sent thee only to give good tidings and to warn. And the Koran have we divided that thou mayest recite it unto men by degrees; and we have sent it down by separate sendings. Say: Believe ye therein or believe ye not; — those verily to whom knowledge hath been given before, when it is told to them, fall down on their faces in adoration, and say, "Extolled be the glory of our Lord! verily the promise of our Lord is accomplished." And they fall down upon their faces weeping, and it increaseth their humility.

Say: Call upon God, or call upon the Merciful, whichever ye call Him by; for His are the goodliest names. And be not loud in thy prayer, nor yet mutter it low; but follow a course between.

And say: Praise be to God who hath not taken a son, and who hath no partner in the Kingdom, and no protector hath He for abasement; and glorify Him gloriously.   [xvii, P]

57

THE ARGUMENTATIVE PERIOD
A.D. 615-622

THE BELIEVER

H. M. The revelation of the Book is from God the Mighty, the Wise, forgiver of sin, and accepter of repentance, — heavy in punishment, long-suffering: there is no God but He, to whom is your journeying. None dispute about the signs of God save those who disbelieve; but let not their traf-

ficking in the land deceive thee. Before them the people of Noah, and the allies after them, denied, and every folk hath purposed against its apostle to overmaster him, and they argued with falsehood to rebut the truth therewith; but I did overmaster them and how great was my punishment! And thus was the sentence of thy Lord accomplished upon those who disbelieved, that they should be inmates of the Fire!

They that bear the Throne and they that are round about it magnify the praise of their Lord and believe in Him and beg forgiveness for those who believe: — "O our Lord! thou embracest all things in mercy and knowledge, give pardon to those who repent and follow thy path, and keep them from the torment of hell, O our Lord, and bring them into the gardens of eternity which thou hast promised to them and to the just among their fathers and their wives and their offspring; verily thou art the Mighty, the Wise; and keep them from evil; for he whom thou keepest from evil on that day, on him hast thou had mercy — the great prize!"

Verily to those who disbelieve shall come a voice, "Surely the hatred of God is greater than your hatred among yourselves, when ye are called to the faith, and disbelieve." They shall say, "O our Lord, twice hast thou given us death, and twice hast thou given us life: and we acknowledge our sins: is there then a way to escape?" — "That hath befallen you because when one God was proclaimed, ye disbelieved: but when Partners were ascribed to Him, ye believed: but judgment belongeth unto God, the High, the Great." It is He who showeth you His signs, and sendeth down to you provision from heaven: but none mindeth except the repentant.

Then call on God with due obedience, though loth be the infidels; of high degree, Lord of the throne; He sendeth down the Spirit at His will upon whom He pleaseth of His servants to warn men of the days of the Tryst: — the day when they shall come forth, and when nothing of theirs shall be hidden from God. Whose is the kingship on that day? It is God's, the

One, the Conqueror! The day every soul shall be rewarded for what it hath earned: no injustice shall there be on that day! Verily God is swift to reckon. And warn them of the approaching Day, when their hearts shall choke in their throats, when the wicked have no friend nor intercessor to prevail. He knoweth the deceitful of eye, and what the breast concealeth, and God judgeth with truth; but those gods whom they call on beside Him cannot judge aught. Verily it is God that heareth and seeth!

Have they not journeyed in the earth, and seen what was the end of those who were before them? Those were mightier than they in strength, and in their footprints on the earth: but God overtook them in their sins, and there were none to keep them from God. That was because apostles had come to them with manifestations, and they believed not: but God overtook them; verily He is strong and heavy in punishment.

We sent Moses of old with our signs and with plain authority, to Pharaoh, and Haman, and Korah: and they said, "A lying wizard." And when he came to them with truth from us they said, "Slay the sons of those who believe with them, and spare their women"; but the plot of the unbelievers was at fault: and Pharaoh said, "Let me alone to kill Moses; and let him call upon his Lord: verily I fear lest he change your religion, or cause iniquity in the earth." And Moses said, "Verily I take refuge with my Lord and your Lord from every one puffed up who believeth not in the day of reckoning." And there spake a man of the family of Pharaoh, a Believer, who concealed his faith, "Will ye kill a man because he saith my Lord is God, when he hath come unto you with manifestations from your Lord? for if he be a liar, upon him alone is his lie, but if he be a man of truth, somewhat of that which he threateneth will befall you. Verily God guideth not him who is an outrageous liar. O my people, today is the kingdom yours who are uppermost in the earth!

but who will defend us against the might of God if it come upon us?" Pharaoh said, "I will only show you what I think, and I will not guide you save in a right way." Then said he who believed, "O my people, verily I fear for you the like of the day of the allies, the like of the state of the people of Noah, and 'Ad, and Thamud, and of those who came after them; and God willeth not injustice to His servants. And, O my people! verily I fear for you the day of crying out: the day when ye shall turn your backs in flight, ye shall have no protector against God; and he whom God misleads, no guide has he. Moreover, Joseph came unto you before with manifestations; but ye ceased not to doubt about the message he brought you, until when he died ye said, 'God will by no means send an apostle after him.' Thus God misleadeth him who is an outrageous doubter. They who dispute about the signs of God, and no proof coming to them, are very hateful to God and to those who believe. Thus God sealeth the heart of all who are puffed up and arrogant." And Pharaoh said, "O Haman, build me a tower, mayhap I shall reach the avenues, the avenues of the heavens, and may ascend to the God of Moses: but verily I hold him a liar." And thus the wickedness of his deed seemed good to Pharaoh, and he was turned away from the right path; but the plot of Pharaoh only came to ruin. And he who believed said, "O my people, follow me: I will guide you the right way. O my people, the life of this world is but a passing joy; but the life to come that is the abode imperishable. Whosoever doeth evil shall not be rewarded save with its like; and whosoever doeth right, whether male or female, being a believer — these shall enter paradise; and be provided therein without count. "And O my people! how is it that I bid you to salvation, but that ye bid me to the Fire? Ye call me to disbelieve in God and join to Him that of which I have no knowledge: and I call you to the Mighty, the Very Forgiving. There is no doubt but that those ye call me to are not to be called on in this world or in the world to come, and that we shall return unto God, and the transgressors shall be inmates of the Fire. Then shall ye call to mind what I said to you: and I commit my case to God: verily God regardeth His servants."

So God kept him from the evil which they devised, and there encompassed the people of Pharaoh the woeful torment — the Fire, to which they shall be exposed morning and evening; and on the day when the Hour cometh — "Enter, ye people of Pharaoh, into the sorest torment." And when they shall wrangle together in the fire, the feeble shall say to those who were puffed up, "Verily we followed you: will ye then remove from us aught of the Fire?" And those who were puffed up will say, "Verily we are all in it. Behold! God hath judged between His servants." And they who are in the Fire shall say to the keepers of Hell, "Call on your Lord, that He remit us one day from the torment." The keepers shall say, "Did there not come to you your apostles with manifestations?" They shall say, "Yea." The keepers shall say, "Call then," but the cry of the unbelievers shall be vain.

Verily we will help our apostles and those who believe, both in the life of this world and on the day when the witness shall stand forth; — a day whereon the excuse of the wicked shall not profit them; but they shall have the curse and the abode of woe. And of old gave we Moses the guidance, and the Children of Israel made we heirs of the Book, — a guidance and a warning to those who have understanding. Be patient, therefore; verily the promise of God is true; and seek pardon for thy sins, and magnify the praises of thy Lord at eve and early morn. Verily those who dispute about the signs of God, without proof reaching them, there is naught in their breasts but pride: and they shall not win. But seek refuge with God; verily, He heareth and seeth. Surely the creation of the heavens and the earth is greater than the creation of man. But most men do not know. Moreover the blind and the seeing are not equal, nor the sinners and the believers,

who do right; — little do they mind! Verily the Hour is assuredly coming: there is no doubt of it; — but most men do not believe. And your Lord saith, "Call upon me; — I will hearken unto you: but as to those who are too puffed up for my service, they shall enter Hell in contempt."

It is God who made you the night to rest in, and the day for seeing: verily God is bounteous to man, but most men are not thankful. That is God your Lord, Creator of all things: there is no god but He: then why do ye turn away? Thus do they turn away who gainsay the signs of God — God, who made you the earth for a resting-place and the heaven for a tent, and formed you and made goodly your forms and provided you with good things — that is God, your Lord. Then blessed be God, the Lord of the worlds! He is the living One. No god is there but He! then call upon Him, purifying your service to Him. Praise be to God, the Lord of the worlds! Say: Verily I am forbidden to serve those ye call on beside God, since there came to me manifestations from my Lord, and I am bidden to resign myself to the Lord of the worlds. He it is who created you of dust, then of a germ, then of blood; then bringeth you forth a babe: then ye come to your strength, then ye become old men (but some of you die before) and reach the appointed term: haply ye will understand it! It is He who giveth life and death; and then He decreeth a thing, He only saith to it, "Be," and it is.

Hast thou not beheld those who cavil at the signs of God, how they are turned aside? They who call the Book, and that with which we have sent our apostles, a lie: they shall soon know! When the shackles shall be on their necks, and the chains, whilst they are dragged into Hell — then in the fire shall they be burned — then shall it be said to them, "Where is that which ye joined in worship beside God?" They shall say, "They are lost to us. Nay! we did not call before upon anything." Thus God misleadeth the unbelievers. That is because ye exulted on earth in what was not true, and because ye were insolent. Enter the gates of Hell to abide therein for ever: and wretched is the abode of the proud!

But be thou patient: verily the promise of God is true: and whether we show thee part of what we threatened them, or whether we make thee to die; yet to us shall they return. We have sent apostles before thee. Of some we have told thee and of some we have not told thee: but no apostle was able to bring a sign unless by the permission of God. But when God's behest cometh, everything is decided with truth: and those perish who think it vain.

It is God who hath made for you the cattle, some to ride and some to eat, (and ye have profit from them) and to attain by them the aims of your hearts, for on them and in ships are ye borne: and He showeth you His signs: which then of the signs of God will ye deny?

Have they not journeyed in the earth, and see what was the end of those who were before them? They were in number more than they, and mightier in strength, and in their footprints on the earth: but what they had earned availed them nothing; and when their apostles came to them with manifestations, they exulted in what knowledge they had; but that which they had scoffed at encompassed them. And when they beheld our might they said, "We believe in God alone, and we disbelieve in what we joined in worship with Him." And naught availed their faith, after they witnessed our might. Such the way of God which was reserved for his servants — and therein the unbelievers have lost. [xl, P]

[THE SOURCES]

SAY ye, We believe in God, and in that which hath been sent down unto us (namely, the Koran), and what hath been sent down unto Abraham (the ten books), and Ishmael, and Isaac, and Jacob, and the tribes, his children, and what Moses received (namely, the Pentateuch), and Jesus (namely the Gos-

63

pel), and what the prophets received from their Lord (namely, books and signs): we make no separation of any of them, believing in some, and disbelieving in some, like the Jews and the Christians; and we resign ourselves unto Him.   [ii, L]

[ADAM AND EVE]

REMEMBER, O Mohammed, when thy Lord said unto the angels, I am about to place in the earth a vicegerent to act for me in the execution of my ordinances therein, namely, Adam, — they said, Wilt Thou place in it one who will corrupt by disobediences, and will shed blood (as did the sons of El-Jann, who were in it; wherefore, when they acted corruptly, God sent to them the angels, who drove them away to the islands and the mountains), when we on the contrary celebrate the divine perfection, occupying ourselves with Thy praise, and extol Thy holiness? Therefore we are more worthy of the vicegerency. — God replied, Verily, I know that which ye know not, as to the affair of appointing Adam vicegerent, and that among his posterity will be the obedient and the rebellious, and the just will be manifest among them. And He created Adam from the surface of the earth, taking a handful of every color that it comprised, which was kneaded with various waters; and He completely formed it, and breathed into it the soul: so it became an animated sentient being. And He taught Adam the names of all things, infusing the knowledge of them into his heart.

Then He showed the things to the angels, and said, Declare unto me the names of these things, if ye say truth in your assertion that I will not create any more knowing than ye, and that ye are more worthy of the vicegerency. They replied, We extol Thy perfection! We have no knowledge excepting what Thou hast taught us; for Thou art the Knowing, the Wise. — God said, O Adam, tell them their names. And when he had told them their names, God said, Did I not say unto you that I know the secrets of the heavens and the earth, and know what ye reveal of your words, saying, Wilt thou place in it, etc., and what ye did conceal of your words, saying, He will not create any more generous towards Him than we, nor any more knowing? [ii, L]

We created you; that is, your father Adam: then we formed you; we formed him, and you in him: then We said unto the angels, Prostrate yourselves unto Adam, by way of salutation; whereupon they prostrated themselves, except Iblees, the father of the jinn, who was amid the angels: he was not of those who prostrated themselves. God said, What hath hindered thee from prostrating thyself, when I command thee? He answered, I am better than he: Thou hast created me of fire, and Thou hast created him of earth. God said, Then descend thou from Paradise; or, as some say, from the heavens; for it is not fit for thee that thou behave thyself proudly therein: so go thou forth: verily thou shalt be of the contemptible. He replied, Grant me respite until the day when mankind shall be raised from the dead. He said, Thou shalt be of those who are respited: (and, in another verse, it is said, until the day of the known period; that is, until the period of the first blast of the trumpet).

And the devil said, Now, as Thou hast led me into error, I will surely lay in wait for the sons of Adam in Thy right way, the way that leadeth to Thee: then I will surely come upon them, from before them, and from behind them, and from their right hands, and from their left, and hinder them from pursuing the way (but, saith Ibn-'Abbas, he cannot come upon them from above, lest he should intervene between the servant and God's mercy), and Thou shalt not find the greater number of them grateful, or believing. God said, Go forth from it, despised and driven away from mercy. Whosoever of them shall follow thee, I will surely fill hell with you all; with thee, and thy offspring, and with men. [vii, L]

And we said, O Adam, dwell thou and thy wife (Howwa or

Eve, whom God created from a rib of his left side) in the garden, and eat ye therefrom plentifully, wherever ye will; but approach ye not this tree, to eat thereof (and it was wheat, or the grape-vine, or some other tree); for if ye do so, ye will be of the number of the offenders. But the devil caused them to slip from the garden, by his saying unto them, Shall I show you the way to the tree of eternity? And he swore to them by God that he was one of the faithful advisers to them: so they ate of it, and He ejected them from that state of delight in which they were. And We said, Descend ye to the earth, ye two with the offspring that ye comprise yet unborn, one an enemy to another; and there shall be for you, in the earth, a place of abode, and a provision of its vegetable produce for a time until the period of the expiration of your terms of life. And Adam learned, from his Lord, words, which were these: — O Lord, we have acted unjustly to our own souls, and if Thou do not forgive us, and be merciful unto us, we shall surely be of those who suffer loss. And he prayed in these words; and He became propitious towards him, accepting his repentance; for He is the Very Propitious, the Merciful. We said, Descend ye from the garden altogether; and if there come unto you from Me a direction (a book and an apostle), those who follow my direction, there shall come no fear on them, nor shall they grieve in the world to come; for they shall enter paradise: but they who disbelieve and accuse our signs of falsehood, these shall be companions of the fire: they shall remain therein for ever. [ii, L]

[ABEL AND CAIN]

RECITE, O Mohammend unto them (that is, to thy people) the history of the two sons of Adam, namely, Abel and Cain, with truth. When they offered their offering to God, Abel's being a ram, and Cain's being produce of the earth, and it was accepted from one of them (that is, from Abel; for fire descended from heaven, and devoured his offering), and it was not accepted from the other, Cain was enraged; but he concealed his envy until Adam performed a pilgrimage, when he said unto his brother, I will assuredly slay thee. Abel said, Wherefore? Cain answered, Because of the acceptance of thine offering to the exclusion of mine. Abel replied, God only accepteth from the pious. If thou stretch forth to me thy hand to slay me, I will not stretch forth my hand to slay thee; for I fear God, Lord of the worlds. I desire that thou shouldest bear the sin thou intendest to commit against me, by slaying me, and thou wilt be of the companions of the fire. And that is the recompense of the offenders.

But his soul suffered him to slay his brother: so he slew him; and he became of the number of those who suffer loss. And he knew not what to do with him; for he was the first dead person upon the face of the earth of the sons of Adam. So he carried him upon his back. And God sent a raven, which scratched up the earth with its bill and its talons and raised it over a dead raven that was with it until it hid it, to show him how he should hide the corpse of his brother. He said, O my disgrace! Am I unable to be like this raven, and to hide the corpse of my brother? — And he became of the number of the repentant. And he digged a grave for him, and hid him. — On account of this which Cain did We commanded the children of Israel that he who should slay a soul (not for the latter's having slain a soul or committed wickedness in the earth, such as infidelity, or adultery, or intercepting the way, and the like) should be regarded as though he had slain all mankind; and he who saveth it alive, by abstaining from slaying it, as though he had saved alive all mankind.   [v, L]

[NOAH AND THE FLOOD]

WE formerly sent Noah unto his people, saying, Verily I am unto you a plain admonisher that ye worship not any but God. Verily I fear for you, if ye worship any other, the pun-

67

ishment of an afflictive day in this world and in the world to come. — But the chiefs who disbelieved among his people replied, We see thee not to be other than a man, like unto us; and we see not any to have followed thee except the meanest of us, the weavers and the cobblers, at first thought or rashly, nor do we see you to have any excellence above us: nay, we imagine you to be a liar in your claims to the apostolic commission. He said, O my people, tell me, if I have an evident proof from my Lord, and He hath bestowed on me the gift of prophecy from Himself which is hidden from you, shall we compel you to receive it when ye are averse thereto? We cannot do so. And, O my people, I ask not of you any riches for delivering my message. My reward is not due from any but God; and I will not drive away those who have believed as ye have commanded me because they are poor people. Verily they shall meet their Lord at the resurrection, and He will recompense them, and will exact for them reparation from those who have treated them with injustice, and driven them away. But I see you to be a people who are ignorant of the end of your case. And, O my people, who will defend me against God if I drive them away? Will ye not then consider? And I do not say unto you, I have the treasures of God; nor do I say, I know the things unseen; nor do I say, Verily I am an angel; nor do I say, of those whom your eyes contemn, God will by no means bestow on them good: (God best knoweth what is in their minds:) verily I should in that case be one of the offenders. — They replied, O Noah, thou hast disputed with us and multiplied disputes with us: now bring upon us that punishment wherewith thou threatenest us, if thou be of those that speak truth. He said, Only God will bring it upon you, if He please to hasten it unto you; for it is His affair, not mine; and ye shall not escape God: nor will my counsel profit you, if I desire to counsel you, if God desire to lead you into error. He is your Lord; and unto Him shall ye be brought back.   [xi, L]

And it was said by revelation unto Noah, Verily there shalt not believe of thy people any but they who have already believed; therefore be not grieved for that which they have done. [xi, L]

And he uttered an imprecation upon them, saying, O my Lord, leave not upon the earth any one of the unbelievers; for if Thou leave them, they will lead Thy servants into error, and will not beget any but a wicked, ungrateful offspring. O my Lord, forgive me and my parents (for they were believers), and whomsoever entereth my house or my place of worship, being a believer, and the believing men, and the believing women, to the day of resurrection and add not to the offenders aught save destruction. [lxxi, L]

And God answered his prayer, and said, Construct the ark in our sight and according to our revelation, and speak not unto Me concerning those who have offended, to beg Me not to destroy them; for they shall be drowned. And he constructed the ark; and whenever a company of his people passed by him, they derided him. He said, If ye deride us, we will deride you, like as ye deride, when we are saved and ye are drowned, and ye shall know on whom shall come a punishment which shall render him vile, and on whom shall befall a lasting punishment. Thus he was employed until when Our decree for their destruction came to pass, and the baker's oven overflowed with water (for this was a signal unto Noah). And We said, Carry into the ark a pair, male and female, of each of these descriptions, (and it is related that God assembled for Noah the wild beasts and the birds and other creatures, and he proceeded to put his hands upon each kind, and his right hand fell always upon the male, and his left upon the female, and he carried them into the ark), and thy family (excepting him upon whom the sentence of destruction hath already been pronounced, namely, Noah's wife, and his son Canaan: but Shem and Ham and Japheth and their three wives he took), and those who have believed;

69

but there believed not with him save a few: they were six men and their wives: and it is said that all who were in the ark were eighty, half of whom were men and half women. And Noah said, Embark ye therein. In the name of God be its course and its mooring. Verily my Lord is very forgiving and merciful. — And it moved along with them amid waves like mountains; and Noah called unto his son, Canaan, who was apart from the ark, O my child, embark with us, and be not with the unbelievers! He replied, I will betake me to a mountain which will secure me from the water. Noah said, There is nought that will secure today from the decree of God any but him on whom He hath mercy. And the waves intervened between them; so he became one of the drowned. And it was said, O earth, swallow up thy water; whereupon it drank it up, except what had descended from heaven, which became rivers and seas, and, O heaven, cease from raining; — and the water abated, and the decree was fulfilled, and the ark rested on El-Joodee, a mountain of El-Jezeeher, near El-Mosil; and it was said, Perdition to the offending people! [xi, L]

And Noah called upon his Lord, and said, O my Lord, verily my son is of my family, and Thou hast promised me to save them, and verily Thy promise is true, and Thou art the most just of those who exercise judgment. God replied, O Noah, verily he is not of thy family who should be saved, or of the people of thy religion. Verily thine asking me to save him is not a righteous act; for he was an unbeliever, and there is no safety for the unbelievers; therefore ask not of me that wherein thou hast no knowledge. I admonish thee, lest thou become one of the ignorant. — Noah said, O my Lord, I beg Thee to preserve me from asking Thee that wherein I have no knowledge; and if Thou do not forgive me and have mercy upon me, I shall be of those who suffer loss. — It was said, O Noah, descend from the ark, with peace from Us, and blessings, upon thee and upon people

that shall proceed from those who are with thee in the ark (that is, their believing posterity); but other people that shall proceed from those who are with thee We will permit to enjoy the provisions of this world; then a painful punishment shall befall them from Us, in the world to come; they being unbelievers. [xi, L]

['AD AND THAMUD]

AND we sent unto the former tribe of 'Ad their brother Hood. He said, O my people, worship God: assert His unity. Ye have no other deity than Him. Will ye not then fear Him, and believe? — The chiefs who disbelieved among his people answered, Verily we see thee to be in a foolish way, and verily we esteem thee one of the liars with respect to the apostolic commission. He replied, O my people, there is no folly in me; but I am an apostle from the Lord of the worlds. I bring unto you the messages of my Lord, and I am unto you a counsellor, intrusted with the apostolic office. Do ye wonder that an admonition hath come unto you from your Lord by the tongue of a man from among you, that he may warn you? And remember how He hath appointed you vicegerents in the earth after the people of Noah, and increased you in tallness of stature. (For the tall among them was a hundred cubits, and the short among them sixty.) Remember, then, the benefits of God, that ye may prosper. They said, Art thou come unto us that we may worship God alone, and relinquish what our fathers worshipped? Then bring upon us that punishment with which thou threatenest us, if thou be of those who speak truth. — He replied, Punishment and indignation from your Lord have become necessary for you. Do ye dispute with me concerning names which ye and your father have given to idols, which ye worship, concerning the worship of which God hath not set down any convincing proof? Then await ye the punishment. I am with you, with those who await it, for your accusing me of falsehood. And the unprofitable wind was sent upon them. But We delivered Hood and them who were with him of the believers by Our mercy; and We cut off the uppermost part of those who charged Our signs with falsehood and who were not believers. [vii, L]

And We sent unto the tribe of Thamud their brother Salih. He said, O my people, worship God. Ye have no other deity than Him. A miraculous proof of my veracity hath come unto you from your Lord, this she-camel of God being a sign unto you. (He had caused her, at their demand, to come forth from the heart of a rock.) Therefore let her feed in God's earth, and do her no harm, lest a painful punishment scize you. And remember how He hath appointed you vicegerents in the earth after the tribe of 'Ad, and given you a habitation in the earth: ye make yourselves, on its plains, pavilions wherein ye dwell in summer, and cut the mountains into houses wherein ye dwell in winter. Remember then the benefit of God, and do not evil in the earth, acting corruptly. — The chiefs who were elated with pride, among his people, said unto those who were esteemed weak, namely, to those who had believed among them, Do ye know that Salih hath been sent unto you from his Lord? They answered, Yea: verily we believe in that wherewith he hath been sent. Those who were elated with pride replied, Verily we disbelieve in that wherein ye have believed. — And the she-camel had a day to water; and they had a day; and they became weary of this. And they hamstrung the she-camel (Kudar the son of Salif doing so by their order and slaying her with the sword); and they impiously transgressed the command of their Lord, and said, O Salih, bring upon us that punishment with which thou threatenest us for killing her, if thou be one of the apostles. And the violent convulsion, a great earthquake, and a cry from heaven, assailed

them, and in the morning they were in their dwellings prostrate and dead. So he turned away from them, and said, O my people, I have brought unto you the message of my Lord and given you faithful counsel; but ye loved not faithful counselors. [vii, L]

[DHU-L-KARNEYN]

THE Jews will ask thee concerning Dhu-l-Karneyn. (His name was El-Iskender, and he was not a prophet.) Answer, I will recite unto you an account of him.

We gave him ability in the earth, by facilitating his journeying therein, and gave him a way to attain everything that he required. And he followed a way towards a place where the sun setteth, until, when he came to the place where the sun setteth, he found that it set in a spring of black mud, as it appeared to the eye; but really that spring was greater than the world; and he found near it a people who were unbelievers. We said, by inspiration, O Dhu-l-Karneyn, either punish the people by slaughter, or proceed against them gently, taking them captive. He said, As to him who offendeth by polytheism, we will punish him by slaughter: then he shall be taken back to his Lord, and He will punish him with a severe punishment, in the fire of hell. But as to him who believeth, and doeth that which is right, he shall have as a reward paradise, and We will say unto him, in Our command, that which will be easy unto him. — Then he followed a way towards the place where the sun riseth, until, when he came to the place where the sun riseth, he found that it rose upon a people (namely, the Zenj) unto whom We had not given anything wherewith to shelter themselves therefrom, neither clothing nor roof; for their land bore no building; but they had subterranean dwellings, into which they retired at sunrise, and they came forth when the sun was high. Thus was the case; and We comprehended with Our Knowledge what were with him (namely, Dhu-l-Karneyn), of weapons and forces and other things. — Then he followed a way until, when he came between the two barriers or mountains, at the confines of the country of the Turks, between which is the barrier of El-Iskender, as will be related presently, he found before them a people who could scarce understand speech. They said, O Dhu-l-Karneyn, verily Gog and Magog are corrupting in the earth, by plunder and tyranny, when they come forth unto us. Shall we therefore pay thee tribute, on the condition that thou make a barrier between us and them?

He answered, the ability which my Lord hath given me, by wealth and other things, is better than your tribute, which I need not. I will make the barrier for you freely: but assist me strenuously by doing that which I desire: I will make between you and them a strong barrier. Bring me pieces of iron of the size of the blocks of stone used in building. — And he built with them, and placed amid them firewood and charcoal, until, when the mass filled up the space between the upper parts of the two mountains, and he had put the bellows and fire around that mass, he said, Blow ye with the bellows. So they blew until, when he had made the iron like fire, he said, Bring me molten brass, that I may pour upon it. And he poured the molten brass upon the heated iron, so that it entered between its pieces and the whole became one mass. And Gog and Magog were not able to ascend to its top by reason of its height and smoothness; nor were they able to perforate it by reason of its hardness and thickness. Dhu-l-Karneyn said, This is a mercy from my Lord: but when the promise of my Lord, as to the eruption of Gog and Magog shortly before the resurrection, shall come to be fulfilled, He will reduce the barrier to dust; and the promise of my Lord concerning their eruption and other events is true. And We will suffer some of them, on that

day, to pour tumultuously among others: and the trumpets shall be blown for the resurrection, and We will gather all creatures together in a body, in one place. And We will set hell, on that day, near before the unbelievers, whose eyes have been veiled from my admonition (the Koran), and who, being blind, have not been directed by it, and who could not hear what the prophet recited unto them, by reason of their hatred of him; wherefore they believed not in him.   [xviii, L]

[ABRAHAM, ISHMAEL AND ISAAC]

REMEMBER when Abraham said to his father A'zar, which was the surname of Terah, Dost thou take images as deities? Verily I see thee and thy people to be in a manifest error. — (And thus, as We showed him the error of his father and his people, did We show Abraham the kingdom of the heavens and the earth, and We did so that he might be of the number of those who firmly believe.) And when the night over-shadowed him, he saw a star that was said to be Venus, and he said unto his people, who were astrologers, This is my Lord, according to your assertion. — But when it set, he said, I like not those that set, to take them as Lords, since it is not meet for a Lord to experience alteration and change of place, as they are of the nature of accidents. Yet this had no effect upon them. And when he saw the moon rising, he said unto them, This is my Lord. — But when it set, he said Verily if my Lord direct me not and confirm me in the right way, I shall assuredly be of the erring people. — This was a hint to his people that they were in error; but it had no effect upon them. And when he saw the sun rising, he said, This is my Lord. This is greater than the star and the moon. — But when it set, and the proof had been rendered more strong to them, yet they desisted not, he said, O my people, verily I am clear of the things which ye associate with God; namely, the images and the heavenly bodies. So they said unto him, What dost thou worship? He answered, Verily I direct my face unto Him who hath created the heavens and the earth, following the right religion, and I am not of the polytheists. — And his people argued with him; but he said, Do ye argue with me respecting God, when He hath directed me, and I fear not what ye associate with Him, unless my Lord will that aught displeasing should befall me? My Lord comprehendeth everything by His knowledge. Will ye not therefore consider? And wherefore should I fear what ye have associated with God, when ye fear not for your having associated with God that of which He hath not sent down unto you a proof? Then which of the two parties is the more worthy of safety? Are we, or you? If ye know who is the more worthy of it, follow him. — God saith, They who have believed, and not mixed their belief with polytheism, for these shall be safe from punishment, and they are rightly directed. [vi, L]

Relate unto them, in the book (that is, the Koran), the history of Abraham. Verily he was a person of great veracity, a prophet. When he said unto his father A'zar, who worshiped idols, O my father, wherefore dost thou worship that which heareth not, nor seeth, nor averteth from thee aught, whether of advantage or of injury? O my father, verily a degree of knowledge hath come unto me, that hath not come unto thee: therefore follow me: I will direct thee into a right way. O my father, serve not the devil, by obeying him in serving idols; for the devil is very rebellious unto the Compassionate. O my father, verily I fear that a punishment will betide thee from the Compassionate, if thou repent not, and that thou wilt be unto the devil an aider, and a companion in hell-fire. — He replied, Art thou a rejecter of my Gods, O Abraham, and dost thou revile them? If thou abstain not, I will assuredly assail thee with stones or with ill words; therefore beware of me, and leave me for a long time. Abraham said, Peace from me be on thee! I will ask pardon for thee

of my Lord; for He is gracious unto me: and I will separate myself from you and from what ye invoke instead of God; and I will call upon my Lord: perhaps I shall not be unsuccessful in calling upon my Lord, as ye are in calling upon idols. — And when he had separated himself from them, and from what they worshiped instead of God, by going to the Holy Land, We gave him two sons, that he might cheer himself thereby, namely, Isaac and Jacob; and each of them We made a prophet; and We bestowed upon them of our mercy, wealth and children; and We caused them to receive high commendation.   [xix, L]

We gave unto Abraham his direction formerly, before he had attained to manhood; and We knew him to be worthy of it. When he said unto his father and his people, What are these images, to the worship of which ye are devoted? — they answered, We found our fathers worshiping them, and we have followed their example. He said unto them, Verily ye and your fathers have been in a manifest error. They said, Hast thou come unto us with truth in saying this, or art thou of those who jest? He answered, Nay, your Lord (the being who deserveth to be worshiped) is the Lord of the heavens and the earth, who created them, not after the similitude of anything pre-existing; and I am of those who bear witness thereof. And, by God, I will assuredly devise a plot against your idols after ye shall have retired, turning your backs. — So, after they had gone to their place of assembly, on a day when they held a festival, he brake them in pieces with an axe, except the chief of them, upon whose neck he hung the axe; that they might return unto the chief and see what he had done with the others. They said, after they had returned and seen what he had done, Who hath done this unto our gods? Verily he is of the unjust. — And some of them said, We heard a young man mention them reproachfully: he is called Abraham. They said, Then bring him before the eyes of the people, that they may bear witness against him of his having done it. They said unto him, when he had been brought, Hast thou done this unto our gods, O Abraham? He answered, Nay, this their chief did it: and ask ye them, if they can speak. And they returned unto themselves, upon reflection, and said unto themselves, Verily we are the unjust, in worshiping that which speaketh not. Then they reverted to their obstinacy, and said, Verily thou knowest that these speak not: then wherefore dost thou order us to ask them? He said, Do ye then worship, instead of God, that which doth not profit you at all, nor injure you if ye worship it not? Fie on you, and on that which ye worship instead of God! Do ye not then understand? — They said, Burn ye him, and avenge your gods, if ye will do so. So they collected abundance of firewood for him, and set fire to it; and they bound Abraham, and put him into an engine, and cast him into the fire. But, saith God, We said, O fire, be thou cold, and a security unto Abraham! So nought of him was burned save his bonds: the heat of the fire ceased, but its light remained; and by God's saying, Security, — Abraham was saved from dying, by reason of its cold. And they intended against him a plot; but he caused them to be the sufferers. And we delivered him and Lot, the son of his brother Haran, from El-'Erak, bringing them unto the land which we blessed for the peoples, by the abundance of its rivers and trees, namely, Syria. Abraham took up his abode in Palestine, and Lot in El-Mu-tekifeh, between which is a day's journey. And when Abraham had asked a son, We gave unto him Isaac, and Jacob as an additional gift, beyond what he had asked, being a son's son; and all of them We made righteous persons and prophets. And We made them models of religion who directed men by Our command unto Our religion; and We commanded them by inspiration to do good works and to perform prayer and to give the appointed alms; and they served Us. And unto Lot We gave judgment and knowledge; and We delivered him from the city which committed filthy actions; for they

were a people of evil, shameful doers; and We admitted him into our mercy; for he was one of the righteous. [xxi, L]

Hast thou not considered him who disputed with Abraham concerning his Lord, because God had given him the kingdom? And he was Nimrod. When Abraham said, (upon his saying unto him, Who is thy Lord, unto whom thou invitest us?), My Lord is He who giveth life and causeth to die, — he replied, I give life and cause to die — And he summoned two men, and slew one of them, and left the other. So when he saw that he understood not, Abraham said, And verily God bringeth the sun from the east: now do thou bring it from the west. — And he who disbelieved was confounded; and God directeth not the offending people. [ii, L]

And Our messengers came formerly unto Abraham with good tidings of Isaac and Jacob, who should be after him. They said, Peace. He replied, Peace be on you. And he tarried not, but brought a roasted calf. And when he saw that their hands touched it not, he disliked them and conceived a fear of them. They said, Fear not: for we are sent unto the people of Lot, that we may destroy them. And his wife Sarah was standing serving them, and she laughed, rejoicing at the tidings of their destruction. And we gave her good tidings of Isaac; and after Isaac, Jacob. She said, Alas! shall I bear a child when I am an old woman, of nine and ninety years, and when this my husband is an old man, of a hundred or a hundred and twenty years? Verily this would be a wonderful thing. — They said, Dost thou wonder at the command of God? The mercy of God and His blessings be on you, O people of the house of Abraham! for He is praiseworthy, glorious. — And when the terror had departed from Abraham, and the good tidings had come unto him, he disputed with Us (that is, with Our messengers) respecting the people of Lot; for Abraham was gentle, compassionate, repentant. And he said unto them, Will ye destroy a city wherein are three hundred believers? They answered, No. He said, And will ye destroy a city wherein are two hundred believers? They answered, No. He said, And will ye destroy a city wherein are forty believers? They answered, No. He said, And will ye destroy a city wherein are fourteen believers? They answered, No. He said, And tell me, if there be in it one believer? They answered, No. He said, Verily in it is Lot. They replied, We know best who is in it. And when their dispute had become tedious, they said, O Abraham, abstain from this disputation; for the command of thy Lord hath come for their destruction, and a punishment not to be averted is coming upon them. [xi, L]

And when Our decree for the destruction of the people of Lot came to be executed, We turned their cities upside-down; for Gabriel raised them to heaven, and let them fall upside-down to the earth; and We rained upon them stones of baked clay, sent one after another, marked with thy Word, each with the name of him upon whom it should be cast: and they are not far distant from the offenders; that is, the stones are not, or the cities of the people of Lot were not, far distant from the people of Mecca. [xi, L]

And Abraham said after his escape from Nimrod, Verily I am going unto my Lord, who will direct me unto the place whither He hath commanded me to go, namely, Syria. And when he had arrived at the Holy Land, he said, O my Lord, give me a son who shall be one of the righteous. Whereupon We gave him the glad tidings of a mild youth. And when he had attained to the age when he could work with him (as some say, seven years; and some, thirteen), he said, O my child, verily I have seen in a dream that I should sacrifice thee, and the dreams of prophets are true; and their actions, by the command of God; therefore consider what thou seest advisable for me to do. He replied, O my father, do what thou art commanded: thou shalt find me, if God please, of the number of the patient. And when they had resigned themselves, and he had laid him down on his temple, in the

valley of Mind, and had drawn the knife across his throat (but it produced no effect, by reason of an obstacle interposed by the divine power), We called unto him, O Abraham, thou hast verified the vision. Verily thus do We reward the well-doers. Verily this was the manifest trial. And We ransomed him whom he had been commanded to sacrifice (and he was Ishmael or Isaac; for there are two opinions) with an excellent victim, a ram from Paradise, the same that Abel had offered: Gabriel (on whom be peace!) brought it, and the lord Abraham sacrificed it, saying, God is most great! And We left this salutation to be bestowed on him by the latter generations, Peace be on Abraham! Thus do We reward the well-doers: for he was of our believing servants.   [xxxvii, L]

Remember when Abraham said, O my Lord, show me how Thou wilt raise to life the dead. — He said, Hast thou not believed? He answered, Yea: but I have asked Thee that my heart may be at ease. He replied, Then take four birds and draw them towards thee, and cut them in pieces and mingle together their flesh and their feathers; then place upon each mountain of thy land a portion of them, then call them unto thee: they shall come unto thee quickly: and know thou that God is mighty and wise. — And he took a peacock and a vulture and a raven and a cock, and did with them as hath been described, and kept their heads with him, and called them; whereupon the portions flew about, one to another, until they became complete: then they came to their heads.   [ii, L]

Remember when his Lord had tried Abraham by certain words, commands and prohibitions, and he fulfilled them, God said unto him, I constitute thee a model of religion unto men. He replied, And of my offspring constitute models of religion. God said, My covenant doth not apply to the offenders, the unbelievers among them. — And when We appointed the house (that is, the Kaabeh) to be a place for the resort of men, and a place of security (a man would meet the slayer of his father there and he would not provoke him

to revenge,) and said, Take, O men, the station of Abraham (the stone upon which he stood at the time of building the House) as a place of prayer, that ye may perform behind it the prayers of the two rek'ahs which are ordained to be performed after the ceremony of the circuiting of the Kaabeh. — And We commanded Abraham and Ishmael, saying, Purify my House and rid it of the idols for those who shall compass it, and those who shall abide there, and those who shall bow down and prostrate themselves. — And when Abraham said, O my Lord, make this place a secure territory (and God hath answered his prayer, and made it a sacred place, wherein the blood of man is not shed, nor is any one oppressed in it, nor is its game hunted or shot, nor are its plants cut or pulled up), and supply its inhabitants with fruits (which hath been done by the transporting of Et-Taif from Syria thither) when the territory of Mecca was desert, without sown land or water, such of them as shall believe in God and the last day. — He mentioned them peculiarly in the prayer agreeably with the saying of God, My covenant doth not apply to the offenders. — God replied, And I will supply him who disbelieveth: I will make him to enjoy a supply of food in this world, a little while: then I will force him, in the world to come, to the punishment of the fire; and evil shall be the transit.

And remember when Abraham was raising the foundations of the House (that is, building it), together with Ishmael, and they said, O our Lord, accept of us our building; for Thou art the Hearer of what is said, the Knower of what is done. O our Lord, also make us resigned unto Thee, and make from among our offspring a people resigned unto Thee, and show us our rites, the ordinances of our worship, and our pilgrimage, and be propitious towards us; for Thou art the Very Propitious, the Merciful. (They begged Him to be propitious to them, notwithstanding their honesty, from a motive of humility, and by way of instruction to their off-

spring.) O our Lord, also send unto them (that is, the people of the House) an apostle from among them (and God hath answered their prayer by sending Mohammed), who shall recite unto them Thy signs (the Koran), and shall teach them the book (the Koran), and the knowledge that it containeth, and shall purify them from polytheism; for Thou art the Mighty, the Wise. — And who will be averse from the religion of Abraham but he who maketh his soul foolish, who is ignorant that it is God's creation, and that the worship of Him is incumbent on it; or who lightly esteemeth it and applieth it to vile purposes; when We have chosen him in this world as an apostle and a friend, and he shall be in the world to come one of the righteous for whom are high ranks? — And remember when his lord said unto him, Resign thyself: — he replied, I resign myself unto the Lord of the worlds. — And Abraham commanded his children to follow the religion; and Jacob, his children; saying, O my children, verily God hath chosen for you the religion of El-Islam; therefore die not without your being Moslems. — It was a prohibition from abandoning El-Islam and a command to persevere therein unto death.   [ii, L]

When the Jews said, Abraham was a Jew, and we are of his religion, — and the Christians said the like, the following was revealed: — O people of the Scripture, wherefore do ye argue respecting Abraham, asserting that he was of your religion, when the Pentateuch and the Gospel were not sent down but after him a long time? Do ye not then understand the falsity of your saying? So ye, O people, have argued respecting that of which ye have knowledge, concerning Moses and Jesus, and have asserted that ye are of their religion: then wherefore do ye argue respecting that of which ye have no knowledge, concerning Abraham? But God knoweth his case, and ye know it not. Abraham was not a Jew nor a Christian: but he was orthodox, a Moslem or one resigned, a unitarian, and he was not of the polytheists.   [iii, L]

[JACOB, JOSEPH AND HIS BRETHREN]

REMEMBER, when Joseph said unto his father, O my father, verily I saw in sleep eleven stars and the sun and the moon: I saw them making obeisance unto me. He replied, O my child, relate not thy vision to thy brethren, lest they contrive a plot against thee, knowing its interpretation to be that they are the stars and that the sun is thy mother and the moon thy father; for the devil is unto man a manifest enemy. And thus, as thou sawest, thy Lord will choose thee, and teach thee the interpretation of events, or dreams, and will accomplish his favor upon thee by the gift of prophecy, and upon the family of Jacob, as He accomplished it upon thy fathers before, Abraham and Isaac; for thy Lord is knowing and wise. — Verily in the history of Joseph and his brethren are signs to the inquirers. — When the brethren of Joseph said, one to another, Verily Joseph and his brother Benjamin are dearer unto our father than we, and we are a number of men; verily our father is in a manifest error; slay ye Joseph, or drive him away into a distant land; so the face of your father shall be directed alone unto you, regarding no other, and ye shall be after it a just people: — a speaker among them, namely, Judah, said, Slay not Joseph, but throw him to the bottom of the well; then some of the travelers may light upon him, if ye do this. And they were satisfied therewith. They said, O our father, wherefore dost thou not intrust us with Joseph, when verily we are faithful unto him? Send him with us tomorrow into the plain, that he may divert himself and sport; and we will surely take care of him. — He replied, Verily your taking him away will grieve me, and I fear lest the wolf devour him while ye are heedless of him. They said, Surely if the wolf devour him, when we are a number of men, we shall in that case be indeed weak. So he sent him with them. And when they went away with him, and agreed to put him at the bottom of the well, they did so.

They pulled off his shirt, after they had beaten him and had treated him with contempt and had desired to slay him; and they let him down; and when he had arrived half-way down the well they let him fall, that he might die; and he fell into the water. He then betook himself to a mass of rock; and they called to him; so he answered them, imagining that they would have mercy upon him. They however desired to crush him with a piece of rock; but Judah prevented them. And We said unto him by revelation, while he was in the well and he was seventeen years of age, or less, to quiet his heart, Thou shalt assuredly declare unto them this their action, and they shall not know thee at the time. And they came to their father at nightfall weeping. They said, O our father, we went to run races, and left Joseph with our clothes, and the wolf devoured him; and thou wilt not believe us, though we speak truth. And they brought false blood upon his shirt. Jacob said unto them, Nay, your minds have made a thing seem pleasant unto you, and ye have done it; but patience is seemly, and God's assistance is implored with respect to that which ye relate.

And travelers came on their way from Midian to Egypt, and alighted near the well; and they sent their drawer of water, and he let down his bucket into the well: so Joseph caught hold upon it, and the man drew him forth; and when he saw him, he said, O good news! This is a young man! — And his brethren thereupon knew his case; wherefore they came upon him, and then concealed his case, making him as a piece of merchandise; for they said, He is our slave who hath absconded. And Joseph was silent, fearing lest they should slay him. And God knew that which they did. And they sold him for a mean price, for some dirhems counted down, twenty, or two-and-twenty; and they were indifferent to him. The travelers then brought him to Egypt, and he who had bought him sold him for twenty denars and a pair of shoes and two garments. And the Egyptian who bought him, namely, Kitfeer, said unto his wife Zeleekha, Treat him hospitably; peradventure he may be advantageous to us, or we may adopt him as a son. For he was childless. And thus We prepared an establishment for Joseph in the land of Egypt, to teach him the interpretation of events, or dreams; for God is well able to effect His purpose; but the unbelievers know not this. And when he had attained his age of strength, thirty years, or three-and-thirty, We bestowed on him wisdom and knowledge in matters of religion, before he was sent as a prophet; for thus do We recompense the well-doers. [xii, L]

And she in whose house he was desired him to yield himself, and she closed the doors and said: "Come, be quick." He replied: "God be my refuge, surely my Lord has given me the best of lodgings. Surely the unjust never prosper." And most surely she resolved to have him and he would have resolved for her had he not seen the power of his Lord. It was thus in order that We might turn evil and indecency from him. Surely he was one of Our devoted servants.

And they both raced for the door, and she rent his shirt from behind, and they both met her husband near the door. She said: "What is the reward of one who wishes evil to thy wife except that he be put in prison or a painful anguish?" He said: "She desired me to yield myself." And a witness from her household bore witness: "If his shirt be torn at the front, then she is truthful and he is a liar. But if his shirt be torn at the back, then she is lying and he is of the truthful." So that when he saw that his shirt was torn from behind, he said: "Surely it is one of your female devices, surely your device is a stupendous one." "O Joseph! turn aside from this. And thou woman ask pardon for thy sin, surely thou art of the sinful ones."

And the women in the city said: "The wife of the minister desires her young man to yield himself to her, she is madly in love with him; surely we see her in an obvious error." So that

89

when she heard of their plan, she sent for them and prepared for them a repast, and she provided each one of them with a knife and said: "Joseph come out in their presence." Therefore when they saw him, they made much of him and cut their hands, and they said: "Holy God, this is no human being. He is nothing but a noble spirit." She said: "He is the one with regard to whom you blamed me, and most surely I desired him to yield himself, but he protected himself. And if he do not what I command him, surely they will put him in prison and he shall be of the dishonored ones."

He said: "My Lord! prison is dearer to me than that they call me to, and if Thou turn not away from me their plan, I shall be attracted towards them and be of those who are ignorant." Therefore God accepted his prayer and turned away from him their plan; surely He is all-Hearing, all-Knowing. Then it appeared to them after they had seen the signs that they should put him in prison for a time.   [xii, s]

And the king said: "Bring him to me." But when the messenger came to him, he said: "Go back to thy lord, then ask him as to the condition of the women who cut their hands. Surely my Lord knows their plan well." He said: "How did it fare with you, when you desired Joseph to yield himself?" They replied: "Holy God! we know no evil of him."

The wife of the minister said: "Nor has the truth come out. It was I who desired him to yield himself and he is of the truthful ones. I say this that he may know I do not lie in his absence, and because God guides not those who are faithless."   [xii, s]

Then it seemed good unto them, after they had seen the signs of his innocence, to imprison him. They will assuredly imprison him for a time, until the talk of the people respecting him cease. So they imprisoned him. And there entered with him into the prison two young men, servants of the king, one of whom was his cup-bearer and the other was his victualer. And they found that he interpreted dreams; wherefore one of them, namely, the cup-bearer, said, I dreamed that I was pressing grapes: and the other said, I dreamed that I was carrying upon my head some bread, whereof the birds did eat: acquaint us with the interpretation thereof; for we see thee to be one of the beneficent. — He replied, There shall not come unto you any food wherewith ye shall be fed in a dream, but I will acquaint you with the interpretation thereof when ye are awake, before the interpretation of it come unto you. This is a part of that which my Lord hath taught me. Verily I have abandoned the religion of a people who believe not in God and who disbelieve in the world to come; and I follow the religion of my fathers, Abraham and Isaac and Jacob. It is not fit for us to associate anything with God. This knowledge of the unity hath been given us of the bounty of God towards us and towards mankind; but the greater number of men are not thankful. O ye two companions and inmates of the prison, are sundry lords better, or is God, the One, the Almighty? Ye worship not, beside Him, aught save names which ye and your father have given to idols, concerning which God hath not sent down any convincing proof. Judgment belongeth not unto any save unto God alone. He hath commanded that ye worship not any but Him. This is the right religion; but the greater number of men know not. O ye two companions of the prison, as to one of you, namely, the cup-bearer, he will serve wine unto his lord as formerly; and as to the other, he will be crucified, and the birds will eat from off his head. — Upon this they said, We dreamed not aught. He replied, The thing is decreed concerning which ye did ask a determination, whether ye have spoken truth or have lied. And he said unto him whom he judged to be the person who should escape of them two, namely the cup-bearer, Mention me unto thy Lord, and say unto him, In the prison is a young man imprisoned unjustly. — And he went forth. But the devil caused him to forget to mention Joseph unto his lord: so he remained

in the prison some years: it is said, seven; and it is said, twelve.

And the king of Egypt, Er-Reiyan the son of El-Weleed said, Verily I saw in a dream seven fat kine which seven lean kine devoured, and seven green ears of corn and seven other ears dried up. O ye nobles, explain unto me my dream, if ye interpret a dream. — They replied, These are confused dreams, and we know not the interpretation of dreams. And he who had escaped, of the two young men, namely the cup-bearer, said (for he remembered after a time the condition of Joseph) I will acquaint you with the interpretation thereof; wherefore send me. So they sent him; and he came unto Joseph, and said, O Joseph, O thou of great veracity, give us an explanation respecting seven fat kine which seven lean kine devoured, and seven green ears of corn and other seven dried up, that I may return unto the king and his companions that they may know the interpretation thereof. He replied, Ye shall sow seven years as usual: (this is the interpretation of the seven fat kine), and what ye reap do ye leave in its ear, lest it spoil; except a little, whereof ye shall eat. Then there shall come, after that, seven grievous years: (this is the interpretation of the seven lean kine), they shall consume what ye shall have provided for them, of the grain sown in the seven years of plenty, except a little which ye shall have kept. Then there shall come, after that, a year wherein men shall be aided with rain, and wherein they shall press grapes and other fruits. — And the king said, when the messenger came unto him and acquainted him with the interpretation of the dream, Bring unto me him who hath interpreted it.

And when he had spoken unto him, he said unto him, Thou art this day firmly established with us, and intrusted with our affairs. What then seest thou fit for us to do? — He answered, Collect provision, and sow abundant seed in these plentiful years, and store up the grain in its ear: then the people will come unto thee that they may obtain provision from thee.

The king said, And who will act for me in this affair? Joseph said, Set me over the granaries of the land; for I am careful and knowing. — Thus did We prepare an establishment for Joseph in the land, that he might take for himself a dwelling therein wherever he pleased. — And it is related that the king crowned him, and put a ring on his finger, and instated him in the place of Kitfeer, whom he dismissed from his office; after which, Kitfeer died, and thereupon the king married him to his wife Zeleekha, and she bore him two sons. We bestow Our mercy on whom We please, and We cause not the reward of the well-doers to perish: and certainly the reward of the world to come is better for those who have believed and have feared.

And the years of scarcity began, and afflicted the land of Canaan and Syria, and the brethren of Joseph came, except Benjamin, to procure provision, having heard that the governor of Egypt gave food for its price. And they went in unto him, and he knew them; but they knew him not: and they spake unto him in the Hebrew language; whereupon he said, as one who distrusted them, What hath brought you to my country? So they answered, For corn. But he said, Perhaps ye are spies. They replied, God preserve us from being spies! He said, Then whence are ye? They answered, From the land of Canaan, and our father is Jacob, the prophet of God. He said, And hath he sons beside you? They answered, Yea: we were twelve; but the youngest of us went away, and perished in the desert, and he was the dearest of us unto him; and his uterine brother remained, and he retained him that he might console himself thereby for the loss of the other. And Joseph gave orders to lodge them, and to treat them generously. And when he had furnished them with their provision, and given them their full measure, he said, Bring me your brother from your father, namely, Benjamin, that I may know your veracity in that ye have said. Do ye not see that I give full measure, and that I am the most hospitable

of the receivers of guests? But if ye bring him not, there shall be no measuring of corn for you from me, nor shall ye approach me. — They replied, We will solicit his father for him, and we will surely perform that. And he said unto his young men, Put their money, which they brought as the price of the corn, in their sacks, that they may know it when they have returned to their family: peradventure they will return to us; for they will not deem it lawful to keep it. — And when they returned to their father, they said, O our father, the measuring of corn is denied us if thou send not our brother unto him; therefore send with us our brother, that we may obtain measure; and we will surely take care of him. He said, Shall I intrust you with him otherwise than as I intrusted you with his brother Joseph before? But God is the best guardian, and He is the most merciful of those who show mercy. — And when they opened their goods, they found their money had been returned unto them. They said, O our father, what desire we of the generosity of the king greater than this? This our money hath been returned unto us; and we will provide corn for our family, and will take care of our brother, and shall receive a camel-load more, for our brother. This is a quantity easy unto the king, by reason of his munificence. — He said, I will by no means send him with you until ye give me a solemn promise by God that ye will assuredly bring him back unto me unless an inevitable and insuperable impediment encompass you. And they complied with this his desire. And when they had given him their solemn promise, he said, God is witness of what we say. And he sent him with them; and he said, O my sons, enter not the city of Misr by one gate; but enter by different gates; lest the evil eye fall upon you. But I shall not avert from you, by my saying this, anything decreed to befall you from God: I only say this from a feeling of compassion. Judgment belongeth not unto any save unto God alone. On Him do I rely, and on Him let those rely who rely.

And when they entered as their father had commanded them, separately, it did not avert from them anything decreed to befall them from God, but only satisfied a desire in the soul of Jacob, which he accomplished; that is, the desire of averting the evil eye, arising from a feeling of compassion: and he was endowed with knowledge, because We had taught him: but the greater number of men, namely the unbelievers, know not God's inspiration of His saints. And when they went in unto Joseph, he received unto him (or pressed unto him) his brother. He said, Verily I am thy brother; therefore be not sorrowful for that which they did from envy to us. And he commanded him that he should not inform them, and agreed with him that he should employ a stratagem to retain him with him. And when he had furnished them with their provision, he put the cup, which was a measure made of gold set with jewels, in the sack of his brother Benjamin. Then a crier cried, after they had gone forth from the chamber of Joseph, O company of travelers, ye are surely thieves. They said (and turned unto them), What is it that ye miss? They answered, We miss the king's measure; and to him who shall bring it shall be given a camel-load of corn, and I am surety for the load. They replied, By God! ye well know that we have not come to act corruptly in the land, and we have not been thieves. The crier and his companions said, Then what shall be the recompense of him who hath stolen it, if ye be liars in your saying, We have not been thieves, — and it be found among you? They answered, His recompense shall be that he in whose sack it shall be found shall be made a slave: he, the thief, shall be compensation for it; namely, for the thing stolen. Such was the usage of the family of Joseph. Thus do We recompense the offenders who are guilty of theft. — So they turned towards Joseph, that he might search their sacks. And he began with their sacks, and searched them before the sack of his brother Benjamin, lest he should be suspected. Then he took forth the measure

95

from the sack of his brother. Thus, saith God, did We contrive a stratagem for Joseph. It was not lawful for him to take his brother as a slave for theft by the law of the king of Egypt (for his recompense by his law was beating, and a fine of twice the value of the thing stolen; not the being made a slave), unless God had pleased, by inspiring him to inquire of his brethren and inspiring them to reply according to their usage. We exalt unto degrees of knowledge and honor whom We please, as Joseph; and there is who is knowing above every one else endowed with knowledge. — They said, If he steal, a brother of his hath stolen before; namely, Joseph; for he stole an idol of gold belonging to the father of his mother, and broke it, that he might not worship it. And Joseph concealed it in his mind, and did not discover it to them. He said within himself, Ye are in a worse condition than Joseph and his brother, by reason of your having stolen your brother from your father and your having treated him unjustly; and God well knoweth what ye state concerning him. — They said, O prince, verily he hath a father, a very old man, who loveth him more than us, and consoleth himself by him for the loss of his son who hath perished, and the separation of him grieveth him; therefore take one of us as a slave in his stead; for we see thee to be one of the beneficent. He replied, God preserve us from taking any save him in whose possession we found our property; for if we took another we should be unjust.

And when they despaired of obtaining him, they retired to confer privately together. The chief of them in age (namely, Reuben) or in judgment (namely, Judah), said, Do ye not know that your father hath obtained of you a solemn promise in the name of God, with respect of your brother, and how ye formerly failed of your duty with respect to Joseph? Therefore I will by no means depart from the land of Egypt until my father give me permission to return to him, or God decide for me by the delivery of my brother; and He is the best, the most just, of those who decide. Return ye to your father, and say, O our father, verily thy son hath committed theft, and we bore not testimony against him save according to that which we knew of a certainty, by our seeing the cup in his sack; and we were not acquainted with what was unseen by us when we gave the solemn promise: had we known that he would commit theft, we had not taken him. And send thou, and ask the people of the city in which we have been, namely, Misr) and the company of travelers with whom we have arrived (who were a people of Canaan): and we are surely speakers of truth. — So they returned to him, and said unto him those words. He replied, Nay, your minds have made a thing seem pleasant unto you, and ye have done it (he suspected them, on account of their former conduct in the case of Joseph); but patience is seemly: peradventure God will bring back Joseph and his brother unto me, together; for He is the Knowing with respect to my case, the Wise in His acts. And he turned from them, and said, O! my sorrow for Joseph! And his eyes became white in consequence of mourning, and he was oppressed with silent grief. They said, By God, thou wilt not cease to think upon Joseph until thou be at the point of death, or be of the number of the dead. He replied, I only complain of my great and unconcealable grief and my sorrow unto God; not unto any beside Him; for He it is unto whom complaint is made with advantage; and I know by revelation from God what ye know not; namely, that the dream of Joseph was true, and that he is living. Then he said, O my sons, go and seek news of Joseph and his brother; and despair not of the mercy of God; for none despaireth of the mercy of God except the unbelieving people.

So they departed towards Egypt, unto Joseph; and when they went in unto him, they said, O Prince, distress and hunger hath affected us and our family, and we have come with paltry money (it was base money, or some other sort): yet give us full measure, and be charitable to us, by excusing the badness of our money; for God recompenseth those who act charitably. And he had pity upon them, and compassion affected him, and he lifted up the curtain that was between him and them: then he said unto them in reproach, Do ye know what ye did unto Joseph, in beating and selling and other actions, and his brother, by your injurious conduct to him after the separation of his brother, when ye were ignorant of what would be the result of the case of Joseph? They replied, after they had recognized him (desiring confirmation), Art thou indeed Joseph? He answered, I am Joseph, and this is my brother. God hath been gracious unto us, by bringing us together; for whosoever feareth God and is patient will be rewarded: God will not suffer the reward of the well-doers to perish. They replied, By God, verily God hath preferred thee above us, and we have been indeed sinners. He said, There shall be no reproach cast on you this day: God forgive you; for He is the most merciful of those that show mercy. And he asked them respecting his father: so they answered, His eyes are gone. And he said, Go ye with this my shirt (it was the shirt of Abraham, which he wore when he was cast into the fire: it was on Joseph's neck appended as an amulet in the well; and it was from paradise: Gabriel commanded him to send it, and said, In it is the odor of paradise, and it shall not be cast upon any one afflicted with a disease but he shall be restored to health), and cast it, said Joseph, upon the face of my father: he shall recover his sight; and bring unto me all your family. — And when the company of travelers had gone forth from El-'Areesh of Egypt, their father said, unto those who were present of his offspring, Verily I perceive the smell of Joseph (for the zephyr had conveyed it to him, by permission of Him whose name be exalted, from the distance of three days' journey, or eight, or more): were it not that ye think I dote, ye would believe me. They replied, By God, thou art surely in thine old error.

And when the messenger of good tidings (namely, Judah)
came with the shirt (and he had borne the bloody shirt;
wherefore he desired to rejoice him, as he had grieved him),
he cast it upon his face, and he recovered his sight. Thereupon Jacob said, Did I not say unto you, I know, from God,
what ye know not? They said, O our father, ask pardon of
our crimes for us; for we have been sinners. He replied, I
will ask pardon for you of my Lord; for He is the Very forgiving, the Merciful. — He delayed doing so until the first
appearance of the dawn, that the prayer might be more likely
to be answered; or, as some say, until the night preceding
Friday.

They then repaired to Egypt, and Joseph and the great men
came forth to meet them; and when they went in unto Joseph,
in his pavilion or tent, he received unto him (or pressed unto
him) his parents (his father and his mother and his maternal
aunt), and said unto them, Enter ye Misr, if God please, in
safety. So they entered; and Joseph seated himself upon his
couch, and he caused his parents to ascend upon the seat of
state, and his parents and his brethren fell down, bowing
themselves unto him (bending, but not putting the fore-
head) upon the ground: such being their mode of obeisance
in that time. And he said, O my father, this is the interpretation of my dream of former times: my Lord hath made it
true; and He had shown favor unto me, since He took me
forth from the prison (he said not, from the well, — from a
motive of generosity, that his brethren might not be abashed),
and hath brought you from the desert, after that the devil
had excited discord between me and my brethren; for my
Lord is gracious unto whom He pleaseth; for He is the Knowing, the Wise. — And his father resided with him four and
twenty years, or seventeen; and the period of his separation
was eighteen, or forty, or eighty years. And death came unto
him; and thereupon he charged Joseph that he should carry
him and bury him by his fathers. So he went himself and

buried him. Then he returned to Egypt and remained after him three and twenty years; and when his case was ended, and he knew that he should not last upon earth, and his soul desired the lasting possession, he said, O my Lord, Thou hast given me dominion, and taught me the interpretation of events or dreams: Creator of the heavens and the earth, Thou art my guardian in this world and in the world to come. Make me to die a Moslem, and join me with the righteous among my forefathers. And he lived after that a week, or more, and died a hundred and twenty years old. And the Egyptians disputed concerning his burial: so they put him in a chest of marble, and buried him in the upper part of the Nile, that the blessing resulting from him might be general to the tracts on each side of it. Extolled be the perfection of Him to whose dominion there is no end! [xii, L]

[JOB]

And remember Our servant Job when he called unto his Lord, Verily the devil hath afflicted me with calamity and pain. (The affliction is attributed to the devil, though all was from God.) And it was said unto him, Strike the earth with thy foot. And he did so; whereupon a fountain of water sprang forth. And it was said, This is cool water for thee to wash with, and to drink. So he washed himself and drank; and every disease that he had, external and internal, quitted him. And We gave unto him his family, and as many more with them (that is, God raised to life for him those of his children who had died, and blest him with as many more), in Our mercy and as an admonition unto those who are endowed with faculties of understanding. And We said unto him, Take in thy hand a handful of dry grass, or of twigs, and strike with it thy wife (for he had sworn that he would inflict upon her a hundred blows, because she had staid away from

him too long one day) and break not thine oath by abstaining from striking her. — So he took a hundred stalks of schoemanthus, or some other plant, and gave her one blow with them. Verily We found him a patient person. How excellent a servant was he! For he was one who earnestly turned himself unto God. [xxxviii, L]

[SHO'EYB]

AND we sent unto Midian their brother Sho'eyb. He said, O my people, worship God; assert His unity. Ye have no other deity but Him. And give not short measure and weight. Verily I see you to be in a state of prosperity that placeth you above the need of doing so; and verily I fear for you, if ye believe not, the punishment of a day that will encompass you with destruction. And, O my people, give full measure and weight with equity; and diminish not unto men aught of their things nor commit injustice in the earth, acting corruptly, by murder or other offenses. The residue of God (His supply that remaineth to you after the completion of the measure) will be better for you than diminution, if ye be believers. And I am not a guardian over you, to recompense you for your actions: I have only been sent as an admonisher. — They replied, in mockery. O Sho'eyb, do thy prayers command thee that we are to leave what our fathers worshiped, or cease to do with our riches what we please? Verily thou art the mild, the right director. This they said in mockery. — He said, O my people, tell me, if I act according to an evident proof from my Lord, and He hath supplied me with a good lawful provision, shall I mix it up with what is forbidden, and shall I not desire to oppose you, and shall I betake myself to that which I forbid you? I desire not aught but your reformation, as far as I am able to effect it, and my help is not in any but in God: on Him do I rely, and unto

Him do I turn me. And, O my people, let not the opposition of me procure for you the befalling you of the like of that which befell the people of Noah or the people of Hood or the people of Salih. And the abodes of the people of Lot are not distant from you: (or the time of their destruction was not long ago): therefore be admonished. And ask ye forgiveness of your Lord, and turn unto Him with repentance; for my Lord is merciful to the believers, loving to them. They replied, O Sho'eyb, we understand not much of what thou sayest, and verily we see thee to be weak among us; and were it not for thy family, we had stoned thee; for thou are not, in our estimation, an honorable person: thy family only are the honorable. He said, O my people, are my family more honorable in your estimation than God, and do ye abstain from slaying me for their sake, and not preserve me for God, and have ye cast Him behind you as a thing neglected? Verily my Lord comprehendeth that which ye do, and He will recompense you. And, O my people, act ye according to your condition: verily I will act according to mine. Ye shall know on whom shall come a punishment that shall render him vile, and who is a liar: and await ye the issue of your case: verily I await with you. — And when Our degree for their destruction came to be executed, we delivered Sho'eyb and those who believed with him, in our mercy, and the cry of Gabriel assailed those who had offended, so that in the morning they were in their abodes prostrate and dead, as though they had not dwelt therein. Was not Midian removed as Thamud had been removed? [xi, L]

JONAH

A. L. R. THESE are the signs of the wise Book! Is it a matter of wonder to the people that we revealed to a man from among themselves, "Warn the people; and bring good tidings to those who believe, that the reward of their good faith is with their Lord?" The unbelievers say, "Lo! this is an evident sorcerer!"

Verily your Lord is God, who made the heavens and the earth in six days — then ascended the throne to govern all things: there is none to plead with Him save by His permission. — This is God, your Lord! then worship ye Him: will ye not mind? Unto Him shall ye all return by the sure promise of God: behold! He produces a creature, then maketh it return again, that He may reward with equity those who believe and do the things that are right: but those who believe not, for them is the scalding drink, and an aching torment — because they did not believe. It is He who hath made the sun for shining, and the moon for light, and ordained him mansions that ye may learn the number of years and the reckoning of time. God did not create that but in truth. He maketh His signs plain to a people who know. Verily in the alterations of the night and the day, and in all that God created in the heavens and the earth, are signs to a godfearing folk.

Verily they who do not hope to meet us, and are satisfied with the life of this world, and are content with it, and they who are careless of our signs, — their dwelling-place is the Fire, for that they have earned. Verily they who believe and do the things that are right, their Lord shall guide them because of their faith; beneath them rivers shall flow in gardens of delight: their cry therein shall be, "Extolled be thy glory, O God!" and their salutation therein shall be "Peace!" And the end of their cry shall be, "Praise to God, Lord of the worlds!" And if God should hasten woe upon men as they fain would hasten weal, verily their appointed term is decreed for them! therefore we leave those who hope not to meet us groping in their disobedience. Moreover, when affliction toucheth man, he calleth us upon his side, sitting, or standing; and when we take away his affliction from him, he passeth on as though he had not called us in the affliction

that touched him! Thus do the deeds of transgressors seem good to them! We have destroyed generations before you, when they sinned and their apostles came to them with manifestations and they would not believe; — thus do we requite the sinful folk. Then we made you their successors in the earth after them, to see how ye would act. But when our manifest signs are recited to them, they who hope not to meet us say, "Bring a different Koran from this, or change it." Say: It is not for me to change it of mine own will. I follow only what is revealed to me: verily I fear if I disobey my Lord the torment of the great Day. Say: If God pleased, I had not recited it to you nor taught it you; and already I had dwelt a lifetime amongst you before that: have ye then no wits? And who is more wicked than he who forgeth a lie against God, or saith His signs are lies? Surely the sinners shall not prosper! And they worship beside God that which cannot hurt them or help them; and they say, "These shall be our pleaders with God." Say: Will ye tell God of anything He doth not know in the heavens and in the earth? Extolled be His glory! and far be He above what they associate with Him! Men were of only one religion: then they differed, and had not a decree gone forth from thy Lord, there had certainly been made a decision between them of that whereon they differed. And they say, "Had a sign been sent down to him from his Lord —" But say: The unseen is with God alone: wait, therefore; verily I am waiting with you. And when we caused men to taste of mercy after affliction had touched them, behold! they have a plot against our signs! Say: God is quick at plotting! verily our messengers write down what ye plot.

He it is who maketh you journey by land and sea, until, when ye are in ships — and they run with them before a fair wind, and they rejoice thereat, there cometh upon them a violent wind, and the waves come upon them from every side, and they suppose they are sore pressed therewith; they call on

God, offering Him sincere religion: — "Do thou but deliver us from this, and we will indeed be of the thankful." But when we have delivered them, lo, they transgress unjustly on the earth! O ye people! ye wrong your own souls only for the enjoyment of the life of this world: then to us shall ye return; and we will tell you what ye have done.

The likeness of the life of this world is as the water which we send down from the heaven, and there mingleth with it the produce of the earth of which men and cattle eat, until when the earth hath put on its blazonry and is arrayed, and its inhabitants think it is they who ordain it, our command cometh to it by night or day, and we make it mown down, as if it had not teemed yesterday! Thus do we explain our signs to a reflecting folk.

And God calleth you unto the abode of peace: and guideth whom He will into the straight way: to those who have done well, weal and to spare, neither blackness shall cover their faces nor shame! these are the inmates of Paradise, to abide therein for ever. And as for those who have earned evil, the recompense of evil is its like; shame shall cover them — no defender shall they have against God — as though their faces were darkened with the gloom of night: these are the inmates of the Fire to abide therein for ever. And on the day we will gather them all together, then will we say to those who made Partners with God, "To your place, ye and your Partners!" and we will separate between them; and their partner shall say, "Ye worshiped not us, and God is witness enough between us and you that we were indifferent to your worship!" Then shall every soul make proof of what it hath sent on before, and they shall be brought back to God their true Master, and what they devised shall vanish from them.

Say: Who provideth you from the heaven and the earth? who is king over hearing and sight? and who bringeth forth the living from the dead and bringeth forth the dead from the

living? and who ruleth all things? And they shall say, "God": then say: Do ye not fear? So that is God your true Lord: and after the truth, what is there but error? How then are ye turned away? Thus is the word of thy Lord fulfilled upon those who work iniquity: they shall not believe. Say: Is there any of the Partners of God who can produce a creature then bring it back again? Say: God produceth a creature, then bringeth it back again: how then are ye deceived? Say: is there any of the Partners who guideth to the truth? Say: God guideth unto the truth. Is he who guideth to the truth the worthier to be followed, or he who guideth not except he be guided? What is in you so to judge? And most of them only follow a fancy: but a fancy profiteth nothing against the truth! verily God knoweth what they do.

Moreover this Koran could not have been devised without God: but it confirmeth what preceded it, and explaineth the Scripture — there is no doubt therein — from the Lord of the worlds. Do they say, "He hath devised it himself?" Say: Then bring a chapter like it: and call on whom ye can beside God, if ye be speakers of truth. Nay, they call all that a lie, of which they compass not the knowledge, though the explanation of it hath not yet been given them; so did those who were before them call the Scriptures lies: but see what was the end of the wicked! And some of them believe in it, and some of them believe not in it. But thy Lord knoweth best about the evildoers. And if they call thee a liar, say, I have my work, and ye have your work: ye are clear of what I work, and I am clear of what ye work. And some of them hearken to thee; but canst thou make the deaf hear if they have no wits? And some of them regard thee; but canst thou guide the blind when they see not? Verily God doth not wrong man a whit, but men wrong themselves.

And on a day He will gather them, as though they had tarried but an hour of the day: they shall know one another! They are lost who denied the meeting with God and were not guided!

Whether we show thee part of what we threatened against them, or whether we take thee to ourself before, to us is their return — then shall God be witness of what they have done. And every nation hath its apostle; and when their apostle is come, it is decided between them with equity, and they are not wronged. Yet they say, "When will this promise be, if ye be speakers of truth?" Say: I have no power for myself for woe or weal, except as God pleaseth. Every people hath its appointed term: when their term is come, they shall not put it off nor hasten it an hour. Say: Bethink ye, if the torment of God come upon you by night or by day, what portion of it will the sinners willingly hasten on? When it happeneth, will we believe it then? Yet would ye fain hasten it on!

Then shall it be said to those who transgressed, "Taste ye the torment of eternity! Shall ye be rewarded save according to what ye have earned?" They would fain know of thee if this is true. Say: Yea, by my Lord, it is indeed true, and ye cannot weaken Him. And if every soul that transgressed owned all that is on earth, he would assuredly give it in ransom; and they will declare their repentance when they have seen the torment: and there shall be a decision betwen them with equity, and they shall not be wronged. Is not indeed whatsoever is in the heavens and the earth God's? Is not indeed the promise of God true? But most of them do not know! He giveth life and death, and to Him shall ye return.

O ye people! now hath a warning come to you from your Lord, and a healing for what is in your breasts, and a guidance and a mercy to the believers. Say: By the grace of God and his mercy! And in that let them therefore rejoice: this is better than what they heap up. Say: Do ye consider what God hath sent down to you for provision: but ye made thereof unlawful and lawful? Say, did God permit you? or do ye forge lies against God? But what will they think on the day of resurrection who forge lies against God? Truly God is full of **bounty** towards man; but most of them are not thankful.

Thou shalt not be in any business, and thou shalt not read from the Koran, and ye shall not do any deed, but we are witness against you when ye are engaged therein; and there escapeth not thy Lord an ant's weight in earth or in heaven: and there is nothing lesser or greater than that, but it is in the plain Book. Are not they truly the friends of God on whom is no fear, neither are they sorrowful — they who believe and feared God, — for them are good tidings in the life of this world, and in the life to come there is no changing in God's sentences. That is the great prize!

And let not their discourse grieve thee: verily all power belongth to God, He it is who heareth and knoweth. Doth not whoever is in the heavens and whoever is in the earth belong to God? then what do they follow who call upon Partners beside God? verily they follow but a fancy; and verily they are naught but liars. It is He who made you the night to rest in, and the day for seeing: verily in that are signs to a folk that can hear!

They say, "God hath taken him a son." Extolled be his glory! He is the Self-sufficient, all that is in the heaven, and all that is in the earth is his! ye have no warranty for this! do ye say about God which ye know not?" Say: Verily they who forge this lie against God shall not prosper: — a passing joy in this world, then to us they return; and then we will make them taste the grievous torment, because they did not believe.

And tell them the story of Noah, when he said to his people, — "O my people! though my dwelling with you and my warning you of the signs of God hath been grievous to you, yet in God do I put my trust: so gather together your case and your Partners; then will not your case fall upon you in the dark: then decide about me and delay not. And if ye turn, yet ask I no reward from you: my reward is with God alone, and I am commanded to be of those who are resigned." But they called him a liar, so we delivered him and those who were with him in the ship, and we made them to survive; and we drowned those who had called our signs lies: see then what was the end of those who were warned!

Then after him, we sent apostles to their people, and they came to them with manifestations: but they would not believe in what they had denied before: thus do we put a seal upon the hearts of the transgressors. Then sent we, after them, Moses and Aaron to Pharaoh and his nobles with our signs; but they were puffed up and were a sinful folk. And when the truth came to them from us, they said, "This is clear sorcery indeed." Moses said, "Say ye of the truth when it is come to you, Is this sorcery? — but sorcerers shall not prosper." They said "Art thou come to us to hinder us from what we found our fathers in, and in order that for you twain there shall be majesty in the land? but we are not going to believe in you!" And Pharaoh said, "Fetch me every wise sorcerer." And when the sorcerers came, Moses said to them, "Cast down what ye have to cast." And when they had cast them down, Moses said, "What ye come with is sorcery: verily God will make it vain; aye, God doth not prosper the work of evildoers; and God will establish the truth by his word, though loth be the sinners."

And none believed in Moses but the children of his own folk, for fear of Pharaoh and his nobles, lest he should afflict them: for of a truth Pharaoh was mighty in the earth, and verily he was of the transgressors. And Moses said, "O my people! if ye believe in God, put your trust in Him, if ye are resigned." And they said, "In God do we put our trust. O our Lord, make us not a trial to the folk of the wicked, and deliver us in Thy mercy from the folk of the unbelievers." Then revealed we to Moses and to his brother: "Build houses for your people in Egypt, and make your houses with a Kibla, and perform prayer, and give good tidings to the believers." And Moses said, "O our Lord, thou hast indeed given to Pharaoh and his nobles adornments and riches in the life of this world: O our Lord! may they err from thy way; O

our Lord, confound their riches, and harden their hearts, so shall they not believe until they see the aching torment." God said: "Your prayer is heard, then stand ye upright, and follow not the path of those who know not." And we brought the Children of Israel across the sea; and Pharaoh and his host followed them, eager and hostile, until when drowning overtook him he said, "I believe that there is no God but He in whom the Children of Israel believe, and I am one of the resigned." "Now! thou hast been rebellious aforetime, and wast one of the evildoers, this day will we raise thee in thy flesh, to be a sign to those who come after thee: but verily many men are heedless of our signs!" Moreover we lodged the Children of Israel in a firm abode, and provided them with good things: and they did not differ until the knowledge came to them; verily thy Lord will decide between them on the Day of Resurrection concerning that on which they differed.

And if thou art in doubt of what we have sent down to thee, inquire of those who read the Scriptures before thee. Now hath truth come unto thee from thy Lord: then be not thou of those who doubt, neither be of those who deny the signs of God lest thou be among the losers. Verily they against whom the word of thy Lord is passed shall not believe, — though there came unto them every kind of sign, — till they behold the aching torment. Else any city had believed, and its faith had benefited it: — save the people of Jonah; when they believed, we took away from them the torment of shame in the life of this world, and provided for them awhile. But if thy Lord pleased, verily all who are in the earth had believed together. Then canst thou compel men to become believers? It is not in a soul to believe but by the permission of God: and He shall lay His curse on those who have no wits. Say: Look upon that which is in the heavens and in the earth: but signs and warners avail not a folk that will not believe! What then can they expect but the like of the days of those who passed away before them? Say: Wait ye, — I too am waiting with you. Then will we deliver our apostles and those who believe: thus is it binding on us to deliver the faithful. Say: O ye people! if ye are in doubt of my religion, I do not worship those whom ye worship beside God; but I worship God, who taketh you away; and I am commanded to be of the faithful. And set thy face towards religion as a Hanif, and be not of those idolators: and invoke not beside God that which can neither help nor hurt; for if they do, thou wilt certainly be of the wicked. And if God touch thee with affliction, there is none to remove it but He. And if He desire thy good, there is none to hinder His bounty — He will confer it on whom He pleaseth of his servants: and He is the Forgiving, the Merciful! Say: O ye people! now hath truth come unto you from your Lord; then he who is guided, is guided only for his own behalf: but he who erreth doth err only against himself; and I am no governor over you! And follow what is revealed to thee: and be patient till God Judgeth; and He is the best of judges.   [x, p]

113

[MOSES AND HIS PEOPLE]

WE will rehearse unto thee, O Mohammed, somewhat of the history of Moses and Pharaoh with truth, for the sake of people who believe. Verily Pharaoh exalted himself in the land of Egypt, and divided its inhabitants into parties to serve him. He rendered weak one class of them, namely the children of Israel, slaughtering their male children, and preserving alive their females, because one of the diviners said unto him, A child will be born among the children of Israel, who will be the means of the loss of thy kingdom; — for he was one of the corrupt doers. And We desired to be gracious unto those who had been deemed weak in the land, and to make them models of religion, and to make them the heirs

of the possessions of Pharaoh, and to establish them in the land of Egypt, and in Syria, and to show Pharaoh and Haman and their forces what they feared from them. And We said, by revelation, unto the mother of Moses, the child above-mention, of whose birth none knew save his sister, Suckle him; and when thou fearest for him cast him in the river Nile, and fear not his being drowned, nor mourn for his separation; for We will restore him unto thee, and will make him one of the apostles. So she suckled him three months, during which he wept not; and then she feared for him, wherefore she put him into an ark pitched within and furnished with a bed for him, and she closed it and cast it in the river Nile by night. And the family or servants of Pharaoh lighted upon him in the ark on the morrow of that night; so they put it before him, and it was opened, and Moses was taken forth from it, suckling milk from his thumb: this happened that he might be unto them eventually an enemy, slaying their men, and an affliction, making slaves of their women; for Pharaoh and Haman (his Wezeer) and their forces were sinners; wherefore they were punished by his hand. And the wife of Pharaoh said, when he and his servants had proposed to kill him, He is delight of the eye unto me and unto thee: do not ye kill him: peradventure he may be serviceable unto us, or we may adopt him as a son. And they complied with her desire; and they knew not the consequence.

And the heart of the mother of Moses, when she knew of his having been lighted upon, became disquieted; and she had almost made him known to be her son, had We not fortified her heart with patience, that she might be one of the believers in Our promise. And she said unto his sister Maryam, Trace him that thou mayest know his case. And she watched him from a distance, while they knew not that she was his sister and that she was watching him. And We forbade him the breasts, preventing him from taking the breast of any nurse except his mother, before his restoration to her: so his sister said, Shall I direct you unto the people of a house who will nurse him for you, and who will be faithful unto him? And her offer was accepted; therefore she brought his mother, and he took her breast: so she returned with him to her house, as God hath said, — And We restored him to his mother, that her eye might be cheerful and that she might not grieve, and that she might know that the promise of God to restore him unto her was true: but the greater number of mankind know not this. And it appeared not that this was his sister and this his mother; and he remained with her until she had weaned him; and her hire was paid for, for every day a deenar, which she took without scruple because it was the wealth of a hostile person. She then brought him unto Pharaoh, and he was brought up in his abode, as God hath related of him in the Chapter of the Poets, where Pharaoh said unto Moses, Have we not brought thee up among us a child, and hast thou not dwelt among us thirty years of thy life?

And when he had attained his age of strength (thirty years or thirty and three), and had become of full age (forty years), We bestowed on him wisdom and knowledge in religion, before he was sent as a prophct; and thus do We reward the well-doers. And he entered the city of Pharaoh, which was Munf, after he had been absent from him a while, at a time when its inhabitants were inadvertent, at the hour of the noon-sleep, and he found therein two men fighting; this being of his party, namely an Israelite, and this of his enemies, an Egyptian, who was compelling the Israelite to carry firewood to the kitchen of Pharaoh without pay: and he who was of his party begged him to aid him against him who was of his enemies. So Moses said unto the latter, Let him go. And it is said that he replied to Moses, I have a mind to put the burden upon thee. And Moses struck him with his fist, and killed him. But he intended not to kill him; and he

buried him in the sand. He said, This is of the work of the devil, who hath excited my anger; for he is an enemy unto the son of Adam, a manifest misleader of him. He said, in repentance, O my Lord, verily I have acted injuriously unto mine own soul, by killing him; therefore forgive me. So he forgave him: for He is the Very Forgiving, the Merciful. — He said, O my Lord, by the favors with which Thou hast favored me, defend me, and I will by no means be an assistant to the sinners after this. — And the next morning he was afraid in the city, watching for what might happen unto him on account of the slain man; and lo, he who had begged his assistance the day before was crying out to him for aid against another Egyptian. Moses said unto him, Verily thou art a person manifestly in error, because of that which thou hast done yesterday and today. But when he was about to lay violent hands upon him, he said, O Moses, dost thou desire to kill me, as thou killedst a soul yesterday? Thou desirest not aught but to be an oppressor in the land, and thou desirest not to be one of the reconcilers — And the Egyptian heard that: so he knew that the killer was Moses; wherefore he departed unto Pharaoh and acquainted him therewith, and Pharaoh commanded the executioners to slay Moses, and they betook themselves to seek him. But a man who was a believer of the family of Pharaoh came from the furthest part of the city, running by a way that was nearer than the way by which they had come: he said, O Moses, verily the chiefs of the people of Pharaoh are consulting respecting thee, to slay thee; therefore go forth from the city: verily I am unto thee one of the admonishers. So he went forth from it in fear, watching in fear of pursuer. He said, O my Lord, deliver me from the unjust people of Pharaoh! And when he was journeying towards Medyen, which was the city of Sho'eyb, eight days' journey from Misr (named after Medyen the son of Abraham), and he knew not the way unto it, he said, Peradventure my Lord will direct me unto the right way, or the middle way. And God sent unto him an angel, having in his hand a short spear; and he went with him thither. And when he came unto the well of Medyen, he found at it a company of men watering their animals; and he found besides them two women keeping away their sheep from the water. He said unto the two women, What is the matter with you that ye water not? They answered, We shall not water until the pastors shall have driven away their animals; and our father is a very old man, who cannot water the sheep. And he watered for them from another well near unto them, for which he lifted a stone that none could lift but ten persons. Then he retired to the shade of an Egyptian thorn-tree on account of the violence of the heat of the sun; and he was hungry, and he said, O my Lord, verily I am in need of the good provision which Thou shalt send down unto me. And the two women returned unto their father in less time than they were accustomed to do: so he asked them the reason thereof; and they informed him of the person who had watered for them; whereupon he said unto one of them, Call him unto me.

And one of them came unto him, walking bashfully, with the sleeve of her shift over her face, by reason of her abashment at him: she said, My father calleth thee, that he may recompense thee with the reward of thy having watered for us. And he assented to her call, disliking in his mind the receiving of the reward: but it seemeth that she intended the compensation if he were of such as desired it. And she walked before him; and the wind blew her garment, and her legs were discovered: so he said unto her, Walk behind me and direct me in the way. And she did so, until she came unto her father, who was Sho'eyb, on whom be peace! and with him was prepared a supper. He said unto him, Sit and sup. But he replied, I fear lest it be a compensation for my having watered for them, and we are a family who seek not a compensation for doing good. He said, Nay, it is my custom and

118

hath been the custom of my fathers to entertain the guest and to give food. So he ate; and acquainted him with his case. And when he had come unto him, and had related to him the story of his having killed the Egyptian and their intention to kill him and his fear of Pharaoh, he replied, Fear not: thou hast escaped from the unjust people. (For Pharaoh had no dominion over Medyen.)

One of the women said (she was the one who had been sent), O my father, hire him to tend our sheep in our stead; for the best thou canst hire is the strong, the trustworthy. So he asked her respecting him, and she acquainted him with what hath been above related, his lifting up the stone of the well, and his saying unto her, Walk behind me; — and moreover, that when she had come unto him, and he knew of her presence, he hung down his head and raised it not. He therefore said, Verily I desire to marry thee unto one of these my two daughters, on the condition that thou shalt be a hired servant to me, to tend my sheep, eight years; and if thou fulfill ten years, it shall be of thine own will; and I desire not to lay a difficulty upon thee by imposing as a condition the ten years: thou shalt find me, if God please, one of the just, who are faithful to their covenants. He replied, This be the covenant between me and thee: whichever of the two terms I fulfill, there shall be no injustice against me by demanding an addition thereto; and God is witness of what we say. And the marriage-contract was concluded according to this; and Sho'eyb ordered his daughter to give unto Moses a rod wherewith to drive away the wild beasts from his sheep: and the rods of the prophets were in his possession; and the rod of Adam, of the myrtle of paradise, fell into her hand; and Moses took it, with the knowledge of Sho'eyb. [xxviii, L]

Hath the history of Moses been related to thee? when he saw fire, during his journey from Medyen, on his way to Egypt, and said unto his family, or his wife, Tarry ye here; for I have seen fire: perhaps I may bring you a brand from it, or

find at the fire a guide to direct me in the way. For he had missed the way in consequence of the darkness of the night. And when he came unto it (and it was a bramble-bush), he was called to by a voice saying, O Moses, verily I am thy Lord; therefore pull off thy shoes; for thou art in the holy valley of Tuwa. And I have chosen thee from among thy people; wherefore hearken attentively unto that which is revealed unto thee by Me. Verily I am God: there is no Deity except Me; therefore worship Me, and perform prayer in remembrance of Me. Verily the hour is coming: I will manifest it unto mankind, and its nearness shall appear unto them by its signs, that every soul may be recompensed therein for its good and evil work: therefore let not him who believeth not in it, and followeth his lust, hinder thee from believing in it, lest thou perish. And what is that in thy right hand, O Moses? — He answered, It is my rod, whereon I lean and wherewith I beat down leaves for my sheep that they may eat them; and I have other uses for it, as the carrying of provision and the water-skin, and the driving away of reptiles. He said, Cast it down, O Moses. So he cast it down; and lo, it was a serpent, running along. God said, Take it, and fear it not: we will restore it to its former state. And he put his hand into its mouth; whereupon it became again a rod. And God said, And put thy right hand to thy left arm-pit, and take it forth: it shall come forth white, without evil, (that is, without leprosy; shining like the rays of the sun, dazzling the sight) as another sign, that We may show thee the greatest of our signs of thine apostleship. (And when he desired to restore his hand to its first state, he put it as before described, and drew it forth.) Go as an apostle unto Pharaoh and those who are with him; for he hath acted with exceeding impiety by arrogating to himself divinity. — Moses said, O my Lord, dilate my bosom, that it may bear the message, and make my affair easy unto me, and loose the knot of my tongue (this had risen from his having been burned in his mouth by a

live coal when he was a child) that they may understand my speech when I deliver the message. And appoint unto me a Wezeer of my family, namely Aaron my brother. Strengthen my back by him, and make him a colleague in my affair, that we may glorify Thee much, and remember Thee much; for Thou knowest us.

God replied, Thou hast obtained thy petition, O Moses, and We have been gracious unto thee another time: for as much as We revealed unto thy mother what was revealed, when she gave birth to thee and feared that Pharaoh would kill thee among the others that were born, saying, Cast him into the ark, and then cast him, in the ark, into the river Nile, and the river shall throw him on the shore; then an enemy unto Me and an enemy unto him (namely Pharaoh) shall take him. And I bestowed on thee, after he had taken thee, love from Me, that thou mightest be loved by men, so that Pharaoh and all that saw thee loved thee; and that thou mightest be bred up in Mine eye. Also forasmuch as thy sister Maryam went that she might learn what became of thee, after they had brought nurses and thou hadst refused to take the breast of any one of them, and she said, Shall I direct you unto one who will nurse him? (whereupon her proposal was accepted, and she brought his mother): so We restored thee to thy mother, that her eye might become cheerful and that she might not grieve. And thou slewest a soul, namely the Copt in Egypt, and wast sorry for his slaughter, on account of Pharaoh, and We delivered thee from sorrow; and We tried thee with other trial, and delivered thee from it. And thou stayedst ten years among the people of Medyen, after thou hadst come thither from Egypt, at the abode of Sho'eyb the prophet, and he married thee to his daughter. Then thou camest according to My decree, as to the time of thy mission, when thou hadst attained the age of forty years, O Moses; and I have chosen thee for Myself. Go thou and thy brother unto the people, with My nine signs, and cease ye not to remember Me. Go ye unto Pharaoh; for he hath acted with exceeding impiety, by arrogating to himself divinity, and speak unto him with gentle speech, exhorting him to relinquish that conduct: peradventure he will consider, or will fear God, and repent. — They replied, O our Lord, verily we fear that he may be precipitately violent against us, hastening to punish us, or that he may act with exceeding injustice towards us. He said, Fear ye not; for I am with you: I will hear and will see. Therefore go ye unto him, and say, Verily we are the apostles of thy Lord: therefore send with us the children of Israel unto Syria, and do not afflict them, but cease to employ them in thy difficult works, such as digging and building and carrying the heavy burden. We have come unto thee with a sign from thy Lord, attesting our veracity in asserting ourselves apostles: and peace be on him who followeth the right direction, and may he be secure from punishment. Verily it hath been revealed unto us that punishment shall be inflicted upon him who chargeth with falsehood that wherewith we have come, and turneth away from it. [xx, L]

Then We sent after the apostles before mentioned, who were Sho'eyb and his predecessors, Moses, with Our signs unto Pharaoh and his nobles, and they acted unjustly with respect to them, disbelieving in the signs: but see what was the end of the corrupt doers. And Moses said, O Pharaoh, verily I am an apostle from the Lord of the worlds unto thee. But he charged him with falsehood: so he said, I am right not to say of God aught but the truth. I have come unto you with a proof from your Lord: therefore send with me to Syria the children of Israel. — Pharaoh said unto him, If thou hast come with a sign confirmatory of thy pretension, produce it, if thou be of those who speak truth. So he cast down his rod; and lo, it was a manifest serpent. And he drew forth his hand from his bosom; and lo, it was white and radiant unto the beholders. The nobles of the people of Pharaoh

said, Verily this is a knowing enchanter: he desireth to expel you from your land. What then do ye command? —They answered, Put off for a time him and his brother, and send unto the cities collectors of the inhabitants, that they may bring unto thee every knowing enchanter. And the enchanters came unto Pharaoh. They said, Shall we surely have a reward if we be the party who overcome? He answered, Yea; and verily ye shall be of those who are admitted near unto my person. They said, O Moses, either do thou cast down thy rod, or we will cast down what we have with us. He replied, Cast ye. And when they cast down their cords and their rods, they enchanted the eyes of the men, diverting them from the true perception of them; and they terrified them; for they imagined them to be serpents running; and they performed a great enchantment. And We spake by revelation unto Moses, saying, Cast down thy rod. And lo, it swallowed up what they had caused to appear changed. So the truth was confirmed, and that which they had wrought became vain; and they were overcome there, and were rendered contemptible. And the enchanters cast themselves down prostrate: they said, We believe in the Lord of the worlds, the Lord of Moses and Aaron. Pharaoh said, Have ye believed in Him before I have given you permission? Verily this is a plot that ye have contrived in the city, that ye may cause its inhabitants to go forth from it. But we shall know what shall happen unto you at my hand. I will assuredly cut off your hands and your feet on the opposite sides — the right hand of each and his left foot: then I will crucify you all. —They replied, Verily unto our Lord shall we return, after our death, of whatever kind it be; and thou dost not take vengeance on us but because we believed in the signs of our Lord when they came unto us. O our Lord, pour upon us patience, and cause us to die Moslems! [vii, L]

And Pharaoh said, Let me alone, that I may kill Moses, (for they had diverted him from killing him), and let him call upon his Lord to defend him from me. Verily I fear lest he change your religion, and prevent your worshiping me, or that he may cause corruption to appear in the earth (that is, slaughter, and other offenses). — And Moses said unto his people, having heard this, Verily I have recourse for defense unto my Lord and your Lord from every proud person who believeth not in the day of account. And a man who was a believer, of the family of Pharaoh (it is said that he was the son of his paternal uncle), who concealed his faith, said, Will ye kill a man because he saith, My Lord is God, — when he hath come unto you with evident proofs from your Lord? And if he be a liar, on him will be the evil consequence of his lie; but if he be a speaker of truth, somewhat of that punishment with which he threateneth you will befall you speedily. Verily God directeth not him who is a transgressor, or polytheist, and a liar. O my people, ye have the dominion today, being overcomers in the land of Egypt; but who will defend us from the punishment of God if ye kill his favorite servants, if it come unto us? — Pharaoh said, I will not advise you to do aught save what I see to be advisable, which is, to kill Moses; and I will not direct you save into the right way. And he who had believed said, O my people, verily I fear for you the like of the day of the confederates, the like of the condition of the people of Noah and 'Ad and Thamud and those who have lived after them: and God willeth not injustice unto His servants. And, O my people, verily I fear for you the day of calling (that is, the day of resurrection, when the people of Paradise and those of Hell shall often call one to another). On the day when ye shall turn back from the place of reckoning unto hell, ye shall have no protector against God. And he whom God shall cause to err shall have no director. Moreover, Joseph (who was Joseph the son of Jacob according to one opinion, and who lived unto the time of Moses; and Joseph the son of Abraham the son of Joseph the son of Jacob, according to another opinion) came unto

you before Moses, with evident miraculous proofs; but ye
ceased not to be in doubt respecting that wherewith he came
unto you, until, when he died, ye said without proof God will
by no means send an apostle after him. Thus God causeth
to err him who is a transgressor, or polytheist, and a skeptic.
They who dispute respecting the signs of God, without any
convincing proof having come unto them, their disputing is
very hateful with God and with those who have believed.
Thus God sealeth every heart, and the whole heart, of a proud
contumacious person.

And Pharaoh said, O Haman, build for me a tower, that I may
reach the avenues, the avenues of the heavens, and ascend
unto the God of Moses; but verily I think Moses a liar in his
assertion that he hath any god but myself. And thus the wickedness of his deed was made to seem comely unto Pharaoh,
and he was turned away from the path of rectitude; and the
artifice of Pharaoh ended not save in loss. And he who had
believed said, O my people, follow me: I will direct you into
the right way. O my people, this present life is only a tem-
porary enjoyment; but the world to come is the mansion of
firm continuance. Whosoever doeth evil, he shall not be
recompensed save with the like of it; and whosoever doeth
good, whether male or female, and is a believer, these shall
enter Paradise; they shall be provided for therein without
reckoning. And, O my people, how is it that I invite you unto
salvation, and ye invite me unto the Fire? Ye invite me to
deny God, and to associate with Him that of which I have
no knowledge; but I invite you unto the Mighty, the Very
Forgiving. There is no doubt but that the false gods to the
worship of which ye invite me are not to be invoked in this
world, nor in the world to come, and that our return shall be
unto God, and that the transgressors shall be the companions
of the Fire. And ye shall remember, when ye see the punishment, what I say unto you; and I commit my case unto God;
for God seeth His servants. — This he said when they threat-

ened him for his opposing their religion. Therefore God preserved him from the evils which they had artfully devised (namely slaughter), and a most evil punishment encompassed the people of Pharaoh, with Pharaoh himself; then they shall be exposed to the Fire morning and evening; and on the day when the hour of judgment shall come, it shall be said unto the angels, Introduce the people of Pharaoh into the most severe punishment. [xl, L]

And the nobles of the people of Pharaoh said unto him, Wilt thou let Moses and his people go that they may act corruptly in the earth, by inviting to disobey thee, and leave thee and thy gods? (For he had made for them little idols for them to worship, and he said, I am your Lord and their Lord; — and therefore he said, I am your Lord the Most High.) He answered, We will slaughter their male children and will suffer their females to live: and verily we shall prevail over them. And thus they did unto them; wherefore the children of Israel complained, and Moses said unto his people, Seek aid of God, and be patient; for the earth belongeth unto God: He causeth whomsoever He will of His servants to inherit; and the prosperous end is for those who fear God. They replied, We have been afflicted before thou camest unto us and since thou hast come unto us. He said, Perhaps your Lord will destroy your enemy and cause you to succeed him in the earth, and He will see how ye will act therein. — And We had punished the family of Pharaoh with dearth and with scarcity of fruits, that they might be admonished and might believe. But when good betided them, they said, This is ours: — that is, we deserve it; — and they were not grateful for it; and if evil befell them, they ascribed it to the ill luck of Moses and those believers who were with him. Nay, their ill luck was only with God: He brought it upon them: but the greater number of them know not this. And they said unto Moses, Whatsoever sign thou bring unto us, to enchant us therewith, we will not believe in thee.

So he uttered an imprecation upon-them, and We sent upon them the flood, which entered their houses and reached to the throats of the persons sitting, seven days, and the locusts, which ate their corn and their fruits, and the kummal, or grubs, or a kind of tick, which sought after what the locusts had left, and the frogs, which filled their houses and their food, and the blood in their waters; distinct signs: but they were proud, refusing to believe in them, and were a wicked people. And when the punishment fell upon them, they said, O Moses, supplicate for us thy Lord, according to that which He hath covenanted with thee, namely that He will withdraw from us the punishment if we believe: verily, if thou remove from us the punishment, we will assuredly believe thee, and we will assuredly send with thee the children of Israel. But when We removed from them the punishment until a period at which they should arrive, lo, they brake their promise. Wherefore We took vengeance on them, and drowned them in the sea, because they charged our signs with falsehood and were heedless of them. And We caused the people who had been rendered weak, by being enslaved, to inherit the eastern parts of the earth and its western parts, which we blessed with water and trees, (namely Syria); and the gracious word of thy Lord was fulfilled on the children of Israel, because they had been patient; and We destroyed the structures which Pharaoh and his people had built and what they had erected.   [vii, L]

We brought the children of Israel across the sea, and Pharaoh and his troops pursued them with violence and anger, until, when drowning overtook him, he said, I believe that there is no deity but He in whom the children of Israel believe, and I am one of the Moslems. But Gabriel thrust into his mouth some of the mire of the sea, lest mercy should be granted him, and said, Now thou believest, and thou hast been rebellious hitherto, and wast one of the corrupters. But today we will raise thee with thy lifeless body from the sea, that thou mayest be a sign unto those who shall come after thee. (It is related, on the authority of Ibn-'Abbas, that some of the children of Israel doubted his death; wherefore he was brought forth to them that they might see him.) But verily many men are heedless of Our signs.   [x, L]

And We brought the children of Israel across the sea; and they came unto a people who gave themselves up to the worship of idols belonging to them; whereupon they said, O Moses, make for us a god, an idol for us to worship, like as they have gods. He replied, Verily ye are a people who are ignorant, since ye have requited God's favor towards you with that which ye have said; for that religion in which these are occupied shall be destroyed, and vain is that which they do. He said, Shall I seek for you any other deity than God, when He hath preferred you above the peoples of your time?   [vii, L]

And We caused the thin clouds to shade you from the heat of the sun in the desert, and caused the manna and the quails to descend upon you, and said, Eat of the good things which We have given you for food, and store not up. — But they were ungrateful for the benefit, and stored up; wherefore it was cut off from them. And they injured not Us thereby; but they did injure their own souls.

Remember, O children of Israel, when ye said, O Moses, we will not bear patiently the having one kind of food, the manna and the quails; therefore supplicate for us thy Lord, that He may produce for us somewhat of that which the earth bringeth forth, of its herbs and its cucumbers and its wheat and its lentils and its onions: — he said unto them, Will ye take in exchange that which is worse for that which is better? — But they refused to recede; therefore he supplicated God, and He said, Get ye down into a great city; for ye shall have therein what ye have asked. — And the marks of abjection and poverty were stamped upon them: so these characteristics necessarily belong to them, even if they are rich, as necessarily as the stamped coin belongeth to its die; and they re-

turned with indignation from God. This was because they did disbelieve in the signs of God, and did slay the prophets (as Zechariah and John) unjustly: this was because they rebelled and did transgress.

And remember when Moses asked drink for his people, who had become thirsty in the desert, and We said, Strike with thy rod the stone. (It was the stone that fled away with his garment: it was light, square, like the head of a man, marble or kedhdhan.) Accordingly he struck it; and there gushed out from it twelve fountains, according to the number of the tribes, each tribe of them knowing their drinking-place. And We said unto them, Eat ye and drink of the supply of God, and commit not evil in the earth, acting corruptly.

Remember also when We obtained your bond that ye would do according to that which is contained in the Law, and had lifted up over you the mountain, namely Mount Sinai, pulled it up by the roots and raised it over you when ye had refused to accept the Law, and We said, Receive that which We have given you, with resolution, and remember that which is contained in it, to do according thereto: peradventure ye will fear the Fire, or acts of disobedience. — Then ye turned back after that; and had it not been for the grace of God towards you and His mercy, ye had certainly been of those who perish. And ye know those of you who transgressed on the Sabbath, by catching fish, when We had forbidden them to do so (and they were the people of Eyeh), and We said unto them, Be ye apes, driven away from the society of men — That thereupon they became such, and they perished after three days. — And We made that punishment an example unto those who were contemporary with them and those who came after them, and a warning to the pious.   [ii, L]

And We appointed unto Moses thirty nights, at the expiration of which We would speak to him, on the condition of his fasting during them; and they were the nights of the month of Dhu-l-Kaadeh; and he fasted during them: but when they were ended, he disliked the smell of his breath; so he used a tooth-stick; whereupon God commanded him to fast ten other nights, that He might speak to Him with the odor of his breath, as He whose name he exalted hath said, — and We completed them by adding ten nights of Dhu-l-Hijjeh: so the stated time of his Lord was completed, forty nights. And Moses said unto his brother Aaron, at his departure to the mountain for the private collocution, Be thou my deputy among my people, and act rightly, and follow not the way of the corrupt doers by agreeing with them in acts of disobedience. And when Moses came at Our appointed time, and his Lord spake unto him without an intermediary, he said, O my Lord, show me Thyself, that I may see Thee. He replied, Thou shalt not see Me: but look at the mountain, which is stronger than thou; and if it remain firm in its place, then shalt thou see Me. And when his Lord displayed Himself to the mountain (that is, when there appeared, of His light, half of the tip of His little finger, as related in a tradition which El-Hakim hath verified), He reduced it to powder, leveling it even with the ground around it; and Moses fell down in a swoon. And when he recovered, he said, Extolled be Thy perfection! I turn unto Thee repenting, and I am the first of the believers in my time. — God said unto him, O Moses, I have chosen thee above the people of thy time by honoring thee by My commissions and by My speaking unto thee: therefore receive what I have given thee, and be of those who are grateful. And We wrote for him upon the tables of the Law (which were of the lote-tree of Paradise, or of chrysolite, or of emerald; in number seven, or ten) an admonition concerning every réquisite matter of religion, and a distinct explanation of everything; and said, Therefore receive it with resolution, and command thy people to act according to the most excellent precepts thereof.   [vii, L]

And the people of Moses, after his departure, made of their ornaments (which they had borrowed of the people of Pharaoh),

a calf which Es-Samiree cast for them, and which lowed; for it had the faculty of doing so in consequence of their having put into its mouth some dust taken from beneath the hoof of the horse of Gabriel; and they took it as a god. Did they not see that it spake not to them, nor directed them in the way? They took it as a god, and were offenders. But when they repented, and saw that they had erred, which was after the return of Moses, they said, Verily if our Lord do not have mercy upon us and forgive us, we shall assuredly be of those who perish.   [vii, L]

And Moses returned unto his people enraged against them, exceedingly sorrowful. He said, O my people, did not your Lord promise you a good true promise, that He would give you the Law? But did the time of my absence seem tedious to you, or did ye desire that indignation from your Lord should befall you, and therefore did ye break your promise to me, and abstain from coming after me? — They answered, We did not break our promise to thee of our own authority; but we were made to carry loads of the ornaments of the people of Pharaoh (which the children of Israel had borrowed of them under pretense of requiring them for a wedding, and which remained in their possession), and we cast them into the fire, by order of Es-Samiree.

And in like manner also Es-Samiree cast their ornaments which he had, and some of the dust which he had taken from the traces of the hoofs of the horse of Gabriel; and he produced unto them a corporeal calf of flesh and blood, which lowed, by reason of the dust, the property of which is to give life to that into which it is put; and he had put it, after he had moulded the calf, into its mouth. And Es-Samiree and his followers said, This is your god, and the god of Moses; but he hath forgotten his lord here, and gone to seek him.

God saith, But did they not see that it returned them not an answer, nor was able to cause them hurt or profit? And Aaron had said unto them, before the return of Moses, O my people, ye are only tried by it; and verily your Lord is the Compassionate; therefore follow me, by worshiping Him, and obey my command. They replied, We will by no means cease to be devoted to the worship of it until Moses return unto us. Moses said after his return, O Aaron, what hindered thee, when thou sawest that they had gone astray, from following me? Hast thou then been disobedient to my command, by remaining among them who worshiped another than God? — He answered, O son of my mother, seize me not by my beard (for he had taken hold of his beard with his left hand), nor by the hair of my head (for he had taken hold of his hair with his right hand, in anger). Verily I feared lest if I followed thee (for a company of those who worshiped the calf would inevitably have followed me) thou shouldst say, Thou hast made a division among the children of Israel, and hast not waited for my sentence. Moses said, And what was thy motive for doing as thou hast, O Samiree? He answered, I saw that which they saw not; therefore I took a handful of dust from the foot-marks of the horse of the apostle Gabriel, and cast it into the molten calf; and thus my soul allured me to take a handful of the dust above-mentioned, and to cast it upon that which had no life, that it might have life; and I saw that thy people had demanded of thee that thou wouldst make them a god; so my soul suggested to me that this calf should be their god. Moses said unto him, Then get thee gone from among us, and the punishment for thee during the period of thy life shall be, that thou shalt say unto whomsoever thou shalt see, Touch me not: — (so he used to wander about the desert, and when he touched any one, or any one touched him, they both became affected with a burning fever:) and verily for thee is a threat which thou shalt by no means find to be false. And look at thy god, to the worship of which thou hast continued devoted. We will assuredly burn it: then we will assuredly reduce it to powder and scatter it in the sea. (And Moses, after he had slaughtered it, did this.) Your deity is God only, except whom there is no deity. He comprehendeth all things by His knowledge.   [xx, L]

And they were made to drink down the calf into their hearts, (that is, the love of it mingled with their hearts as drink mingleth) because of their unbelief.

Remember, O children of Israel, when Moses said unto his people who worshiped the calf, O my people, verily ye have injured your own souls by your taking to yourselves the calf as a god; therefore turn with repentance unto your Creator from the worship of it, and slay one another: (that is, let the innocent among you slay the criminal): this will be best for you in the estimation of your Creator. And He aided you to do that, sending upon you a black cloud, lest one of you should see another and have compassion on him, until there were slain of you about seventy thousand. And thereupon He became propitious towards you, accepting your repentance; for He is the Very Propitious, the Merciful.

Remember also, O children of Israel, when ye said, having gone forth with Moses to beg pardon of God for your worship of the calf, and having heard his words, O Moses, we will not believe thee until we see God manifestly: — whereupon the vehement sound assailed you, and ye died, while ye beheld what happened to you. Then We raised you to life after ye had been dead, that peradventure ye might give thanks. [ii, L]

And Moses chose from his people seventy men, of those who had not worshiped the calf, by the command of God, at the time appointed by Us for their coming to ask pardon for their companions' worship of the calf; and he went forth with them; and when the convulsion (the violent earthquake) took them away (because, saith Ibn-'Abbas, they did not separate themselves from their people when the latter worshiped the calf), Moses said, O my Lord, if Thou hadst pleased, Thou hadst destroyed them before my going forth with them, that the children of Israel might have beheld it and might not suspect me; and me also. Wilt Thou destroy us for that which the foolish among us have done? It is naught but Thy trial: Thou wilt cause to err thereby whom Thou pleasest, and Thou wilt rightly guide whom Thou pleasest. Thou art our guardian; and do Thou forgive us and have mercy upon us; for Thou art the best of those who forgive: and appoint for us in this world what is good, and in the world to come; for unto Thee have we turned with repentance. — God replied, I will afflict with My punishment whom I please, and My mercy extendeth over everything in the world; and I will appoint it, in the world to come, for those who fear and give the legal alms, and those who believe on Our signs, who shall follow the apostle, the illiterate prophet, Mohammed, whom they shall find written down with them in the Pentateuch and the Gospel, by his name and his description. He will command them that which is right, and forbid them that which is evil; and will allow them as lawful the good things among those forbidden in their law, and prohibit them the impure, as carrion and other things, and will take off from them their burden and the yokes that were upon them, as the slaying of a soul for an atonement in repentance, and the cutting off of the mark left by impurity. And those who shall believe in him and honor him and assist him and follow the light which shall be sent down with him, namely the Koran, these shall be the prosperous. [vii, L]

And remember when Moses said unto his people, O my people, remember the favor of God towards you, since He hath appointed prophets from among you, and made you masters of servants and other attendants (and given you what He hath not given any other of the peoples, as the manna and the quails and other things. O my people, enter the Holy Land which God hath decreed for you (namely Syria), and turn not back, lest ye turn losers. — They replied, O Moses, verily there is in it a gigantic people, of the remains of the tribe of 'Ad, and we will not enter it until they go forth from it; but if they go forth from it, then we will enter. — There-

upon two men, of those who feared to disobey God (namely Joshua and Caleb, of the chiefs whom Moses sent to discover the circumstances of the giants, and on whom God had conferred favor, and who had concealed what they had seen of the state of the giants, excepting from Moses: wherefore the other chiefs became cowardly) said unto them, Enter ye upon them through the gate of the city, and fear them not; for they are bodies without hearts; and when ye enter it, ye overcome; and upon God place your dependence, if ye be believers. — But they said, O Moses, we will never enter it while they remain therein. Therefore go thou and thy Lord, and fight: for we remain here. — Then Moses said, O my Lord, verily I am not master of any but myself and my brother: therefore distinguish between us and the unrighteous people. — God replied, Verily the Holy Land shall be forbidden them for forty years; they shall wander in perplexity in the land: and be not thou solicitous for the unrighteous people. — The land through which they wandered was only nine leagues in extent. They used to journey during the night with diligence; but in the morning they found themselves in the place whence they had set forth; and they journeyed during the day in like manner. Thus they did until all of them had become extinct, excepting those who had not attained the age of twenty years; and it is said that they were six hundred thousand. Aaron and Moses died in the desert; and mercy was their lot: but punishment was the lot of those. And Moses begged his Lord, when he was about to die, that He would bring him as near as a stone's throw to the Holy Land: wherefore He did so. And Joshua was made a prophet after the forty years, and he gave orders to fight against the giants. So he went with those who were with him, and fought against them: and it was Friday; and the sun stood still for him awhile, until he had made an end of fighting against them.   [v, L]

Karoon was of the people of Moses (he was the son of his paternal uncle, and the son of his maternal aunt, and he believed

in him); but he behaved insolently towards them; for We had bestowed upon him such treasures that their keys were heavy burdens for a company of men endowed with strength, in number, as some say, seventy; and some, forty; and some, ten; and some, another number. Remember when his people, the believers among the children of Israel, said unto him, Rejoice not exultingly in the abundance of thy wealth; for God loveth not those who so rejoice; but seek to attain, by means of the wealth which God hath given thee, the latter abode of Paradise, by expending thy wealth in the service of God; and neglect not thy part in this world, to work therein for the world to come; but be beneficent unto mankind, by bestowing alms, as God hath been beneficent unto thee; and seek not to act corruptly in the earth; for God loveth not the corrupt doers. He replied, I have only been given it on account of the knowledge that I possess. For he was the most learned of the children of Israel in the Law, after Moses and Aaron. God saith, Did he not know that God had destroyed before him, of the generations, those that were mightier than he in strength and who had amassed more abundance of wealth? And the wicked shall not be asked respecting their sins, because God knoweth them: they shall be sent into the Fire without a reckoning.

And Karoon went forth unto his people in his pomp, with his many dependents mounted, adorned with garments of gold and silk, upon decked horses and mules. Those who desired the present life said, O would that we had the like of that which hath been bestowed on Karoon in this world! Verily he is possessed of great good fortune! — But those unto whom knowledge of what God hath promised in the world to come had been given, said unto them, Woe to you! The reward of God in the world to come (which is Paradise) is better for him who believeth and worketh righteousness than that which hath been bestowed on Karoon in the present world; and none shall receive it but the patient in the service of God.

And We caused the earth to cleave asunder and swallow up him and his mansion, and he had no forces to defend him, in the place of God, nor was he of the number of the saved. And the next morning, those who had wished for his place the day before said, Aha! God enlargeth provision unto whom he pleaseth of His servants, and is sparing of it unto whom he pleaseth! Had not God been gracious unto us, He had caused the earth to cleave asunder and swallow up us! Aha! the ungrateful for His benefits do not prosper!   [xxviii, L]

Remember, O children of Israel, when Moses said unto his people (when one of them had been slain, whose murderer was not known, and they asked him to beg God that He would discover him to them, wherefore he supplicated Him), Verily God commandeth you to sacrifice a cow. They said, Dost thou make a jest of us? He said, I beg God to preserve me from being one of the foolish. So when they knew that he decidedly intended what he had ordered, they said, Supplicate for us thy Lord, that He may manifest to us what she is; that is, what is her age. Moses replied, He saith, She is a cow neither old nor young; but of a middle age, between those two: therefore do as ye are commanded. They said, Supplicate for us thy Lord, that He may manifest to us what is her color. He replied, He saith, She is a red cow: her color is very bright: she rejoiceth the beholders.

They said, Supplicate for us thy Lord, that He may manifest to us what she is, whether she be a pasturing or a working cow; for cows of the description mentioned are to us like one another; and we, if God please, would be rightly directed to her. He replied, He saith, She is a cow not subdued by work that plougheth the ground, nor doth she water the field: she is free from defects and the marks of work; there is no color in her different from the rest of her color. They said, Now thou hast brought the truth. And they sought her, and found her in the possession of a young man who acted piously towards his mother, and they bought her for as much gold as her hide would contain. Then they sacrificed her; but they were near to leaving it undone, on account of the greatness of her price. And when ye slew a soul, and contended together respecting it, We said, Strike the slain person with part of her. So he was struck with her tongue, or the root of her tail, or, as some say, with her right thigh; whereupon he came to life, and said, Such-a-one and such-a-one slew me, — to the two sons of his uncle. And he died. They two the murderers were therefore deprived of the inheritance, and were slain. Thus God raiseth to life the dead, and showeth you the proof of His power, that peradventure ye may understand, and know that He who is able to raise to life one soul is able to raise to life many souls. Then your hearts became hard, O ye Jews, so as not to accept the truth, after that, and they were as stones, or more hard: for of stones there are indeed some from which rivers gush forth; and of them there are indeed some that cleave asunder and water issueth from them; and of them there are indeed some that fall down through fear of God; whereas your hearts are not impressed, nor do they grow soft, nor do they become humble. But God is not heedless of that which ye do: He only reserveth you unto your time.   [ii, L]

El-Bukharee hath related that Moses performed the office of a preacher among the children of Israel, and was asked who was the most knowing of men; to which he answered, I: — whereupon God blamed him for this, because he did not refer the knowledge thereof to Him. And God said unto him by revelation, Verily I have a servant at the place where the two seas meet, and he is more knowing than thou. Moses said, O my Lord, and how shall I meet with him? He answered, Thou shalt take with thee a fish, and put it into a measuring-vessel, and where thou shalt lose the fish, there is he. So he took a fish, and put it into a vessel. Then he departed, and Joshua the son of Nun departed with him, until they came to the rock, where they laid down their heads and slept. And the fish became agitated in the vessel, and escaped from it, and

fell into the sea, and it made its way in the sea by a hollow passage, God withholding the water from the fish so that it became like a vault over it: and when Moses' companion awoke, he forgot to inform him of the fish.

142 And when they had passed beyond that place, and proceeded until the time of the morning-meal on the following day, Moses said unto his young man, Bring us our morning-meal: we have experienced fatigue from this our journey. He replied, What thinkest thou? When we repaired to the rock to rest at that place, I forgot the fish, and none made me forget to mention it but the devil; and it made its way in the sea in a wonderful manner. — Moses said, Our loss of the fish is what we were desiring; for it is a sign unto us of our finding him whom we seek. And they returned by the way that they had come, following the footsteps, and came to the rock. And they found one of Our servants (namely El-Khidr) unto whom We had granted mercy from Us (the gift of prophecy, in the opinion of some, and the rank of a saint, according to another opinion which most of the learned hold), and whom We had taught knowledge from Us respecting things unseen.

Moses said unto him, namely El-Khidr, Shall I follow thee, that thou mayest teach me part of that which thou hast been taught, for a direction unto me? He answered, Verily thou canst not have patience with me. For how canst thou be patient with respect to that whereof thou comprehendest not the knowledge? — He replied, Thou shalt find me, if God please, patient; and I will not disobey any command of thine. He said, Then if thou follow me, ask me not respecting anything: but be patient until I give thee an account thereof.

And Moses assented to his condition. And they departed, walking along the shore of the sea, until, when they embarked in the ship that passed by them, El-Khidr made a hole in it, by pulling out a plank or two planks from it on the outside by means of an axe when it reached the middle of the sea. Moses said unto him, Hast thou made a hole in it that thou mayest drown its people? Thou hast done a grievous thing. He replied, Did I not say that thou couldst not have patience with me? Moses said, Chastise me not for my forgetfulness, nor impose on me a difficulty in my case. — And they departed, after they had gone forth from the vessel, walking on, until, when they found a boy who had not attained the age of knowing right and wrong, playing with other children, and he was the most beautiful of them in countenance, and El-Khidr slew him, Moses said unto him, Hast thou slain an innocent soul, without his having slain a soul? Thou hast done an iniquitous thing. — He replied, Did I not say that thou couldst not have patience with me? Moses said, If I ask thee concerning anything after this time, suffer me not to accompany thee. Now hast thou received from me an excuse for thy separating thyself from me. — And they departed and proceeded until, when they came to the people of a city (which was Antioch), they asked food of its people; but they refused to entertain them: and they found therein a wall, the height whereof was a hundred cubits, which was about to fall down; whereupon El-Khidr set it upright with his hand. Moses said unto him, If thou wouldst, thou mightest have obtained pay for it, since they did not entertain us, notwithstanding our want of food. El-Khidr said unto him, This shall be a separation between me and thee; but before my separation from thee, I will declare unto thee the interpretation of that which thou couldst not bear with patience.

As to the vessel, it belonged to ten poor men, who pursued their business on the sea; and I desired to render it unsound; for there was behind them a king, an unbeliever, who took every sound vessel by force. And as to the boy, his parents were believers, and we feared that he would transgress against them rebelliously and impiously: for, according to a tradition related by Moslem, he was constituted by nature an unbeliever, and had he lived he had so acted; wherefore we desired that their Lord should create for them a better than he in virtue,

143

and one more disposed than he to filial piety. And God created for them a daughter, who married a prophet, and gave birth to a prophet, by means of whom God directed a people to the right way. And as to the wall, it belonged to two orphan youths in the city, and beneath it was a treasure buried, of gold and silver, belonging to them; and their father was a righteous man; and thy Lord desired that they should attain their age of strength and take forth their treasure through the mercy of thy Lord. And I did what hath been mentioned not of mine own will, but by direction of God. This is the interpretation of that which thou couldst not bear with patience.   [xviii, L]

[SAUL, DAVID, SOLOMON]

HAST thou not considered the assembly of the children of Israel after the death of Moses, when they said unto a prophet of theirs, namely Samuel, Set up for us a king, under whom we will fight in the way of God? He said unto them, If fighting be prescribed as incumbent on you, will ye, peradventure, abstain from fighting? They replied, And wherefore should we not fight in the way of God, since we have been expelled from our habitations and our children by their having been taken prisoners and slain? — The people of Goliath had done thus unto them. — But when fighting was commanded them, they turned back, excepting a few of them, who crossed the river with Saul, as will be related. And God knoweth the offenders. And the prophet begged his Lord to send a king; whereupon he consented to send Saul. And their prophet said unto them, Verily God hath set up Saul as your king. They said, How shall he have the dominion over us, when we are more worthy of the dominion than he, (for he was not of the royal lineage, nor of the prophetic, and he was a tanner, or a tender of flocks or herds), and he hath not been endowed with ample wealth? He replied, Verily God hath chosen him as king over you, and increased him in largeness of knowledge and of body, (for he was the wisest of the children of Israel at that time, and the most comely of them, and the most perfect of them in make), and God giveth his kingdom unto whom He pleaseth; and God is ample in His beneficence, knowing with respect to him who is worthy of the kingdom. — And their prophet said unto them, when they demanded of him a sign in proof of his kingship, Verily the sign of his kingship shall be that the ark shall come unto you (in it were the images of the prophets: God sent it down unto Adam, and it passed into their possession; but the Amalekites took it from them by force: and they used to seek victory thereby over their enemy, and to advance it in the fight, and to trust in it, as He — whose name be exalted! — hath said); therein shall be tranquility from your Lord, and relics of what the family of Moses and the family of Aaron have left: namely, the two sandals of Moses, and his rod, and the turban of Aaron, and a measure of the manna that used to descend upon them, and the fragments of the tables of the Law: the angels shall bear it. Verily in this shall be a sign unto you of his kingship, if ye be believers. Accordingly the angels bore it between heaven and earth, while they looked at it, until they placed it by Saul; whereupon they acknowledged his kingship, and hastened to the holy war; and Saul chose of their young men seventy thousand.

And when Saul went forth with the troops from Jerusalem, and it was violently hot weather, and they demanded of him water, he said, Verily God will try you by a river, that the obedient among you, and the disobedient, may appear, (and it was between the Jordan and Palestine), and whoso drinketh thereof, he is not of my party (but he who tasteth not thereof, he is of my party), excepting him who taketh forth a draught in his hand, and is satisfied therewith, not adding to it; for he is of my party; — then they drank thereof abundantly, excepting a few of them, who were content only with the handful of

water. It is related that it sufficed them for their own drinking and for their beasts, and they were three hundred and somewhat more than ten. And when he had passed over it, he and those who believed with him, those who had drunk plentifully said, We have no power today to contend against Goliath and his troops.

And they were cowardly, and passed not over it. They however who held it as certain that they should meet God at the resurrection (and they were those who had passed over it) said, How many a small body of men hath overcome a great body by the permission of God! And God is with the patient, to defend and aid. — And when they went forth to battle against Goliath and his troops, they said, O our Lord, pour upon us patience, and make firm our feet, by strengthening our hearts for the holy war, and help us against the unbelieving people! — And they routed them by the permission of God, and David who was in the army of Saul, slew Goliath. And God gave David the kingship over the children of Israel, and prophecy, after the death of Samuel and Saul, and these two gifts had not been given together to any one before him; and He taught him what He pleased, as the art of making coats of mail, and the language of birds. And were it not for God's repelling men, one by another, surely the earth had become corrupt by the predominance of the polytheists and the slaughter of the Moslems and the ruin of the places of worship: but God is beneficent to the peoples, and hath repelled some by others.   [ii, L]

Hath the story of the two opposing parties come unto thee, O Mohammed, when they ascended over the walls of the oratory of David, having been prevented going in unto him by the door, because of his being engaged in devotion? When they went in unto David, and he was frightened at them, they said, Fear not: we are two opposing parties. It is said that they were two parties of more than one each; and it is said that they were two individuals, angels, who came as two litigants, to admonish David, who had ninety-nine wives, and had desired the wife of a person who had none but her, and married her and taken her as his wife. One of them said, One of us hath wronged the other; therefore judge between us with truth, and be not unjust, but direct us into the right way. Verily this my brother in religion, had nine-and-ninety ewes, and I had one ewe; and he said, Make me her keeper. And he overcame me in the dispute.—And the other confessed him to have spoken truth.—David said, Verily he hath wronged thee in demanding thy ewe to add her to his ewes; and verily many associates wrong one another, except those who believe and do righteous deeds: and few indeed are they. — And the two angels said, ascending in their proper or assumed forms to heaven, The man hath passed sentence against himself. So David was admonished. And David perceived that We had tried him by his love of that woman; wherefore he asked pardon of his Lord, and fell down prostrating himself, and repented. So We forgave him that; and verily for him was ordained an increase of good fortune in this world, and an excellent retreat in the world to come.   [xxxviii, L]

We compelled the mountains to glorify Us, with David and the birds also, on his commanding them to do so, when he experienced languor; and We did this. And We taught him the art of making coats of mail (for before his time plates of metal were used) for you among mankind in general, that they might defend you from your suffering in warring with your enemies. —Will ye then, O people of Mecca, be thankful for My favors, believing the apostles? — And We subjected unto Solomon the wind, blowing strongly, and being light at his desire, which ran at his command to the land that We blessed (named Syria); and We knew all things (knowing that what We gave him would stimulate him to be submissive to his Lord). And We subjected, of the devils, those who should dive for him in the sea and bring forth from it jewels for him, and do other work besides that; that is, building, and perform-

147

ing other services; and We watched over them, that they might not spoil what they executed; for they used, when they had finished a work before night, to spoil it, if they were not employed in something else. [xxi, L]

We gave unto David Solomon his son. How excellent a servant was he! For he was one who earnestly turned himself unto God, glorifying and praising Him at all times. Remember when, in the latter part of the day, after the commencement of the declining of the sun, the mares standing on three feet and touching the ground with the edge of the fourth foot, swift in the course, were displayed before him. They were a thousand mares, which were displayed before him after he had performed the noon-prayers, on the occasion of his desiring to make use of them in a holy war; and when nine hundred of them had been displayed, the sun set, and he had not performed the afternoon-prayers. So he was grieved, and he said, Verily I have preferred the love of earthly goods above the remembrance of my Lord, so that the sun is concealed by the veil. Bring the horses back unto me. Therefore they brought them back. And he began to sever with his sword the legs and the necks, slaughtering them, and then cutting off their legs, as a sacrifice unto God, and gave their flesh in alms; and God gave him in compensation what was better than they were and swifter, namely the wind, which traveled by his command whithersoever he desired.

And We tried Solomon by depriving him of his kingdom. This was because he married a woman of whom he became enamored, and she used to worship an idol in his palace without his knowledge. His dominion was in his signet; and he pulled it off once and deposited it with his wife, who was named El-Emeeneh; and a jinnee came unto her in the form of Solomon, and took it from her. And We placed upon his throne a counterfeit body; namely that jinnee, who was Sakhr, or another. He sat upon the throne of Solomon, and the birds and other creatures surrounded him; and Solomon went forth, with a changed appearance, and saw him upon his throne, and said unto the people, I am Solomon:—but they denied him. Then he returned unto his kingdom, after some days, having obtained the signet and put it on, and seated himself upon his throne. He said, O my Lord, forgive me, and give me a dominion that may not be to any one beside me; for Thou art the Liberal Giver. So We subjected unto him the wind, which ran gently at his command whithersoever he desired; and the devils also, every builder of wonderful structures, and divers that brought up pearls from the sea, and others bound in chains which connected their hands to their necks. And We said unto him, This is Our gift, and bestow thou thereof upon whomsoever thou wilt, or refrain from bestowing, without rendering an account. And verily for him was ordained a high rank with Us, and an excellent retreat.   [xxxviii, L]

We bestowed on David and Solomon knowledge in judging men and in the language of the birds and other matters; and they said, Praise be to God who hath made us to excel many of His believing servants, by the gift of prophecy and by the subjection of the jinn and mankind and the devils. And Solomon inherited from David the gift of prophecy and knowledge; and he said, O men, we have been taught the language of the birds, and have had bestowed on us of everything wherewith prophets and kings are gifted. Verily this is manifest excellence. — And his armies of jinn and men and birds were gathered together unto Solomon, and they were led on in order, until, when they came unto the valley of ants, (which was at Et-Taif, or in Syria, the ants whereof were small or great) an ant the queen of the ants, having seen the troops of Solomon, said: O ants, enter your habitations, lest Solomon and his troops crush you violently, while they perceive not. And Solomon smiled, afterwards laughing at her saying, which he heard from the distance of three miles, the wind conveying it to him: so he withheld his forces when he came in sight of their valley, until the ants had entered their dwellings:

and his troops were on horses and on foot in this expedition. And he said, O my Lord, inspire me to be thankful for Thy favor which Thou hast bestowed upon me and upon my parents, and to do righteousness which Thou shalt approve, and admit me, in Thy mercy, among Thy servants, the righteous, the prophets and the saints.

And he examined the birds, that he might see the lapwing, that saw the water beneath the earth, and directed to it by pecking the earth, whereupon the devils used to draw it forth when Solomon wanted it to perform the ablution for prayer; but he saw it not: and he said, Wherefore do I not see the lapwing? Is it one of the absent? — And when he was certain of the case he said, I will assuredly punish it with a severe punishment, by plucking out its feathers and its tail and casting it in the sun so that it shall not be able to guard against excessive thirst; or I will slaughter it; or it shall bring me a manifest convincing proof showing its excuse. — And it tarried not long before it presented itself unto Solomon submissively, and raised its head and relaxed its tail and its wings: so he forgave it; and he asked it what it had met with during its absence; and it said, I have become acquainted with that wherewith thou hast not become acquainted, and I have come unto thee from Sheba (a tribe of El-Yemen) with a sure piece of news. I found a woman reigning over them, named Bilkees, and she hath been gifted with everything that princes require, and hath a magnificent throne. (Its length was eighty cubits; and its breadth, forty cubits; and its height, thirty cubits: it was composed of gold and silver set with fine pearls and with rubies and chrysolites, and its legs were of rubies and chrysolites and emeralds: upon it were closed seven doors: to each chamber through which one passed to it was a closed door.) I found her and her people worshiping the sun instead of God, and the devil hath made their works to seem comely unto them, so that he hath hindered them from the right way, wherefore they are not rightly directed to the worship of God, who produceth what is hidden (namely the rain and vegetables) in the heavens and the earth, and knoweth what mankind and others conceal in their hearts, and what they reveal with their tongues. God: there is no deity but He, the Lord of the magnificent throne, between which and the throne of Bilkees is a vast difference. Solomon said to the lapwing, We will see whether thou hast spoken truth or whether thou art of the liars. Then the lapwing guided them to the water, and it was drawn forth by the devils; and they quenched their thirst and performed the ablution and prayed. Then Solomon wrote a letter, the form whereof was this: — From the servant of God, Solomon the son of David, to Bilkees the queen of Sheba. In the name of God, the Compassionate, the Merciful. Peace be on whomsoever followeth the right direction. After this salutation, I say, Act ye not proudly towards me; but come unto me submitting. — He then sealed it with musk, and stamped it with his signet, and said unto the lapwing, Go with this my letter and throw it down unto Bilkees and her people: then turn away from them, but stay near them, and see what reply they will return. So the lapwing took it, and came unto her, and around her were her forces; and he threw it down into her lap; and when she saw it, she trembled with fear. Then she considered what was in it, and she said unto the nobles of her people, O nobles, an honorable sealed letter hath been thrown down unto me. It is from Solomon; and it is this: — In the name of God, the Compassionate, the Merciful. Act ye not proudly towards me: but come unto me submitting. — She said, O nobles, advise me in mine affair. I will not decide upon a thing unless ye bear me witness. — They replied, We are endowed with strength and endowed with great valor; but the command belongeth to thee; therefore see what thou wilt command us to do, and we will obey thee. She said, Verily kings, when they enter a city, waste it, and render the mighty of its inhabitants abject; and thus will they do who have sent the letter. But I will send unto them with a gift, and I will see

with what the messengers will return, whether the gift will be accepted, or whether it will be rejected. If he be merely a king, he will accept it; and if he be a prophet, he will not accept it. — And she sent male and female servants, a thousand in equal numbers, five hundred of each sex, and five hundred bricks of gold, and a crown set with jewels, and musk and amergris and other things, by a messenger with a letter. And the lapwing hastened unto Solomon, to tell him the news; on hearing which, he commanded that bricks of gold and silver should be cast, and that a horse-course should be extended to the length of nine leagues from the place where he was, and that they should build around it a wall with battlements, of gold and silver, and that the handsomest of the beasts of the land and of the sea should be brought with the sons of the jinn on the right side of the horse-course and on its left.

And when the messenger came with the gift, and with him his attendants, unto Solomon, Solomon said, Do ye aid me with wealth? But what God hath given me (namely the gift of prophecy and the kingdom) is better than what He hath given you, of worldly goods; yet ye rejoice in your gift, because ye glory in the showy things of this world. Return unto them with the gift that thou hast brought; for we will surely come unto them with forces with which they have not power to contend, and we will surely drive them out from their country, Sheba, abject and contemptible, if they come not unto us submitting. And when the messenger returned unto her with the gift, she placed her throne within seven doors, within her palace; and her palace was within seven palaces; and she closed the doors, and set guards to them, and prepared to go unto Solomon, that she might see what he would command her to do. She departed with twelve thousand kings, each king having with him many thousands, and proceeded until she came as near to him as a league's distance; when he knew of her approach, he said, O nobles, which of you will bring unto me her throne before they come unto me submitting?

An'efreet, of the jinn, answered, I will bring it unto thee before thou shalt arise from thy place wherein thou sittest to judge from morning until midday; for I am able to do it, and trustworthy with respect to the jewels that it compriseth and other matters. Solomon said, I desire it more speedily. And thereupon he with whom was knowledge of the revealed scripture (namely his Wezeer Asaf the son of Barkhiya), who was a just person, acquainted with the most great name of God, which ensured an answer to him who invoked thereby, said, I will bring it unto thee before thy glance can be withdrawn from any object. And he said unto him, Look at the sky. So he looked at it; then he withdrew his glance, and found it placed before him: for during his look towards the sky, Asaf prayed, by the most great name, that God would bring it; and it so happened, the throne passing under the ground until it came up before the throne of Solomon. And when he saw it firmly placed before him, he said, This is the favor of my Lord, that He may try me, whether I shall be thankful or whether I shall be unthankful. And he who is thankful is thankful for the sake of his own soul, which will have the reward of his thankfulness; and as to him who is ungrateful, my Lord is independent and bountiful.

Then Solomon said, Alter ye her throne so that it may not be known by her, that we may see whether she be rightly directed to the knowledge thereof, or whether she be of those who are not rightly directed to the knowledge of that which is altered. He desired thereby to try her intelligence. So they altered it, by adding to it, or taking from it, or in some other manner. And when she came, it was said unto her, Is thy throne like this? She answered, As though it were the same. (She answered them ambiguously like as they had questioned her ambiguously, not saying, Is this thy throne? — and had they so said, she had answered, Yes.) And when Solomon saw her knowledge, he said, And we have had knowledge bestowed on us before her, and have been Moslems. But what she wor-

153

shiped instead of God hindered her from worshiping Him; for she was of an unbelieving people. — It was said unto her also, Enter the palace. (It had a floor of white, transparent glass, beneath which was running water, wherein were fish. Solomon had made it on its being said unto him that her legs and feet were hairy like the legs of an ass. And when she saw it, she imagined it to be a great water, and she uncovered her legs, that she might wade through it; and Solomon was on his throne at the upper end of the palace, and he saw that her legs and her feet were handsome. He said unto her, Verily it is a palace evenly spread with glass. And he invited her to embrace El-Islam, whereupon she said, O my Lord, verily I have acted unjustly towards mine own soul, by worshiping another than Thee, and I resign myself, with Solomon, unto God, the Lord of the worlds. And he desired to marry her; but he disliked the hair upon her legs; so the devils made for him the depilatory of quick-lime, wherewith she removed the hair, and he married her; and he loved her, and confirmed her in her kingdom. He used to visit her every month once, and to remain with her three days; and her reign expired on the expiration of the reign of Solomon. It is related that he began to reign when he was thirteen years of age, and died at the age of three and fifty years. Extolled be the perfection of Him to the duration of whose dominion there is no end.   [xxvii, L]
We subjected unto Solomon the wind, which traveled in the morning (unto the period when the sun began to decline) the distance of a month's journey, and in the evening (from the commencement of the declining of the sun into its setting) a month's journey. And We made the fountain of molten brass to flow from him three days with their nights in every month, as water floweth; and the people worked until the day of its flowing, with that which had been given unto Solomon. And the jinn were those who worked in his presence, by the will of his Lord; and such of them as swerved from obedience to Our command We will cause to taste of

the punishment of hell in the world to come (or, as it is said by some, We cause to taste of its punishment in the present world, an angel beating them with a scourge from hell, the stripe of which burneth them). They made for him whatever he pleased, of lofty halls, with steps whereby to ascend to them, and images (for they were not forbidden by his law), and large dishes, like great tanks for watering camels, around each of which assembled a thousand men, eating from it, and cooking-pots standing firmly on their legs, cut out from the mountains in El-Yemen, and to which they ascended by ladders. And We said, Work, O family of David, in the service of God, with thanksgiving unto Him for what He hath given you: — but few of My servants are the thankful. And when We decreed that Solomon should die, and he died, and remained standing, and leaning upon his staff for a year, dead, the jinn meanwhile performing those difficult works as they were accustomed to do, not knowing of his death, until the worm ate his staff, whereupon he fell down; nothing showed them his death but the eating reptile that ate his staff. And when he fell down, the jinn plainly perceived that if they had known things unseen (of which things was the death of Solomon), they had not continued in the ignominious affliction of their difficult works, imagining that he was alive, inconsistently with their opinion that they knew things unseen. And that the period was a year was known by calculating what the worm had eaten of his staff since his death in each day and night or other space of time. [xxxiv, L]

157

[JONAH]

VERILY Jonah was one of the apostles. Remember when he fled unto the laden ship, being angry with his people, because the punishment wherewith he had threatened them did not fall upon them; wherefore he embarked in the ship; and it became stationary in the midst of the sea: so the sailors said, Here is

a slave who hath fled from his master, and the lot will discover him: — and he cast lots with those who were in the ship, and he was the one upon whom the lot fell. They therefore cast him into the sea, and the fish swallowed him; and he was reprehensible, for having gone to the sea, and embarked in the ship, without the permission of his Lord. And had he not been of those who glorified God (by his saying often in the belly of the fish, There is no God but Thou! I extol Thy perfection! Verily I have been of the offenders!) he had remained in his belly until the day of resurrection. And We cast him on the plain land, the same day, or after three or seven days, or twenty or forty days; and he was sick; and We caused a gourd plant to grow up over him, to shade him. It had a trunk, contrary to what is the case of gourds in general, being miraculously produced for him. And a wild she-goat came to him evening and morning, of whose milk he drank until he became strong. And We sent him after that, as before, unto his people in Nineveh, in the land of El-Mosil, a hundred thousand, or they were a greater number by twenty or thirty or seventy thousand; and they believed on beholding one punishment wherewith they had been threatened; wherefore We allowed them enjoyment of their goods for a time, until the expiration of their terms of life. [xxxvii, L]

[EZRA]

HAST thou not considered him who passed by a city (which was Jerusalem), riding upon an ass, and having with him a bsaket of figs and a vessel of the juice of grapes (and he was 'Ozeyr), and it was falling down, even its roofs, Nebuchadnezzar having ruined it? He said, wondering at the power of God, How will God quicken this after its death? — And God caused him to die for a hundred years. Then he raised him to life: and He said unto him, How long hast thou tarried here?

— He answered I have tarried a day, or part of a day. — For he slept in the first part of the day, and was deprived of his life, and was reanimated at sunset. He said Nay, thou hast tarried a hundred years: but look at thy food and thy drink: they have not become changed by time: and look at thine ass. — And he beheld it dead, and its bones white and shining. — We have done this that thou mayest know, and that We may make thee a sign of the resurrection unto men. And look at the bones of thine ass, how We will raise them; then We will clothe them with flesh. — So he looked at them, and they had become put together, and were clothed with flesh, and life was breathed into it, and it brayed. Therefore when it had been made manifest to him he said, I know that God is able to accomplish everything.   [ii, L]

[THE MESSIAH]

REMEMBER when the wife of 'Imran said, (when she had become aged, and desired offspring, wherefore she supplicated God, and became sensible of pregnancy), O my Lord, verily I devote unto Thee what is in my womb, to be dedicated to the service of Thy holy house: then accept it from me; for Thou art the Hearer of prayer, the Knower of intentions. And 'Imran perished while she was pregnant. And when she gave birth to her daughter although she was hoping that it might be a boy; since none but boys were dedicated, she said, O my Lord, verily I have brought forth a female, (and God well knew what she had brought forth), and the male is not as the female, the latter not being fit for the service of the temple; and I have named her Mary; and I beg thy protection for her and her offspring from the accursed devil. (In the traditions it is said, No child is born but the devil hath touched it at the time of its birth, wherefore it first raiseth its voice by crying, excepting Mary and her son.) And her Lord accepted Mary

from her mother with a gracious acceptance, and caused her to grow with an excellent growth, as though she grew in a day as a child generally groweth in a month. Her mother took her to the doctors, the keepers of the Holy House, and said, Receive ye this devoted child. And they eagerly desired her, because she was the daughter of their chief. But Zechariah said, I am more worthy of having her; for her maternal aunt is with me. They however replied, Nay, but we will cast lots. — So they departed (and they were nine and twenty) to the river Jordan, and cast their divining arrows on the understanding that he whose arrow should become steady in the water and rise should be acknowledged most worthy of her; and the arrow of Zechariah became steady, and he took her, and built for her a chamber in the temple, with stairs to which no one ascended but himself. And he used to bring her her food and her drink and her ointment; and used to find with her the fruits of winter in summer, and the fruits of summer in winter, as He — whose name be exalted! — hath said. And Zechariah maintained her. Whenever Zechariah went in to her in the chamber, he found with her provisions. He said, O Mary, whence came to thee this? She answered, (being then a little child), It is from God: He bringeth it to me from Paradise: for God supplieth whom He pleaseth without reckoning.

Then, when he saw this, and knew that He who was able to produce a thing out of its season was able to give a child in old age, (and the people of his house had become extinct), Zechariah supplicated his Lord, when he had entered the chamber to pray in the latter part of the night. He said, O my Lord, give me from Thee a good offspring, a righteous son; for Thou art the Hearer of prayer. — And the angels (by which is meant Gabriel) called to him as he stood praying in the chamber of the temple, saying, God promiseth thee John, who shall be a verifier of the Word which cometh from God, (that is, Jesus; for he is the Spirit of God, and was named the Word because he was created by the word Be), and a chief, and one followed, and chaste, and a prophet, of the righteous. (It is related that he neither did any sin nor intended any.) — He said, O my Lord, how shall I have a son, when old age hath come upon me, when I have attained the utmost age, a hundred and twenty years, and my wife is barren, and hath attained the age of eight and ninety? — He answered, It shall be thus. God will do what He pleaseth. — Zechariah said, O my Lord, give me a sign. — He replied, Thy sign shall be that thou shalt not speak unto men for three days, except by signal; but remember thy Lord often, and glorify Him in the evening and in the morning. [iii, L]

And he went forth unto his people from the chamber, and made a sign unto them, as though he would say Glorify God in the morning and in the evening as usual. And he knew by his being prevented from speaking unto them that his wife had conceived John. And after his birth, by some years, God said unto him, O John, receive the book (that is, the Law) with resolution. And We bestowed on him wisdom (the gift of prophecy) when he was yet a child, three years of age, and compassion from Us for mankind, and a disposition to bestow alms upon them. And he was pious, and dutiful to his parents, and was not proud or rebellious toward his Lord; and peace from Us was on him on the day when he was born, and on the day of his death, and shall be on the day when he shall be raised to life. [xix, L]

And remember when the angels (that is, Gabriel) said, O Mary, verily God hath chosen thee and hath purified thee and hath chosen thee above the women of the peoples of thy time. O Mary, be devout towards thy Lord and prostrate thyself and bow down with those who bow down: pray with those who pray. — This is one of the announcements of things unseen by thee: We reveal it unto thee, O Mohammed; for thou wast not with them when they cast their divining arrows that it might appear to them which of them should rear Mary, and thou wast not with them when they disputed together as

to rearing her. — Remember when the angels (that is Gabriel) said, O Mary, verily God promiseth thee the Word from Him, whose name shall be the Messiah, Jesus the son of Mary, honorable in this world by his prophetic office, and in the world to come by his intercession and high stations, and of those admitted near unto God; and he shall speak unto men in the cradle, and when of full age, and he shall be of the righteous. — She said, O my Lord, how shall I have a son, when a man hath not touched me? — He answered, It shall be thus; God will create what He pleaseth: when He determineth a thing, He only saith unto it, Be, — and it is. And He will teach him writing and wisdom and the Law and the Gospel, and constitute him an apostle to the children of Israel, in youth or after adolescence. And Gabriel breathed into the bosom of her shift; whereupon she conceived; and those events of her history which are related in the Soorat Maryam happened. [iii, L]

Relate in the book (that is, the Koran) the history of Mary, when she retired from her family to a place towards the east, in the house, and she took a veil to conceal herself from them; and We sent unto her our spirit Gabriel, and he appeared unto her as a perfect man. She said, I beg the Compassionate to preserve me from thee! If thou be a pious person, thou wilt withdraw from me. — He replied, I am only the messenger of thy Lord to inform thee that He will give thee a pure son, endowed with the gift of prophecy. She said, How shall I have a son, when a man hath not touched me, and I am not a harlot? He answered, Thus shall it be: a son shall be created unto thee without a father. Thy Lord saith, This is easy unto Me; and thus shall it be that We may make him a sign unto men, showing Our power, and a mercy from Us unto him who shall believe in him: for it is a thing decreed. — And she conceived him; and she retired with him yet unborn to a distant place far from her family; and the pains of childbirth urged her to repair to the trunk of a palm-tree that she might lean against it. And she gave birth to the child, which was conceived and formed and born in an hour. She said, Oh! would that I had died before this event, and had been a thing forgotten and unnoticed! — But he who was below her (namely Gabriel, who was on a lower place than she) called to her, Grieve not. God hath made below thee a rivulet: and shake thou towards thee the trunk of the palm-tree (which was dried-up); it shall let fall upon thee ripe dates, fresh-gathered: therefore eat of the dates, and drink of the water of the rivulet, and be of cheerful eye on account of the child: and if thou see any one of mankind, asking thee concerning the child, say, I have vowed unto the Compassionate an abstinence from speech with mankind respecting him and other matters; therefore I will not speak today unto a man after this.

163

And she brought the child unto her people, carrying him. They said, O Mary, thou hast done a strange thing. O sister of Aaron, (he was a righteous man; and the meaning is, O thou who art like him in chastity), thy father was not a man of wickedness, nor was thy mother a harlot. Then whence gottest thou this child? — And she made a sign to them, pointing towards him, namely the child, as though she would say, Speak ye unto him. They said, How shall we speak unto him who is in the cradle, an infant? He however said, Verily I am the servant of God: He hath given me the book of the Gospel, and hath appointed me a prophet; and He hath made me blessed wherever I shall be, and hath commanded me to observe prayer and give alms as long as I shall live, and hath made me dutiful to my mother, and hath not made me proud or wicked. And peace from God was on me on the day when I was born, and will be on the day when I shall die, and on the day when I shall be raised to life.

This was Jesus the son of Mary. I have spoken the saying of truth, concerning which the Christians doubt, for they say that Jesus is the son of God. It is not meet for God to get a

son. Extolled be His purity from that imputation! When He decreeth a thing that He desireth to bring into existence, He only saith unto it, Be, — and it is: and thus He created Jesus the son of Mary without a father.—And say, Verily God is my Lord and your Lord: therefore worship ye Him: this is a right way, leading to Paradise. But the Christians have differed among themselves concerning Jesus, as to whether he be the son of God, or a deity with Him, or the third of three. And woe unto them who have disbelieved in that which hath been stated, or in other matters, on account of the assembly of a great day, the day of resurrection, and its terrors. How will they hear, and how will they see, on the day when they shall come unto Us in the world to come! But the offenders in the present world are in a manifest error: they are deaf, so that they hear not the truth; and blind, so that they see it not. And do thou, O Mohammed, warn the unbelievers of Mecca of the day of sighing (the day of resurrection, when the evil-doer shall sigh for his having neglected to do good in the present world), when the command for their punishment shall be fulfilled, while they in the present world are in a state of heedlessness with respect to it, and while they believe not therein. Verily We shall inherit the earth and whomsoever are upon it (the heedless and others; they being destroyed); and unto Us shall they be brought back to be recompensed.   [xix, L]

And when God sent Jesus to the children of Israel, he said unto them, Verily I am the apostle of God unto you; for I have come unto you with a sign from your Lord; for I will make for you of earth the similitude of a bird, and will breathe into it, and it shall be a bird, by the permission of God; (and he made for them a bat; for it is the most perfect of birds in make; and it flew while they looked at it; but when it had gone out of their sight, it fell down dead); and I will cure the blind from his birth, and the leper; (and he cured in one day fifty thousand, by prayer, on the condition of faith); and I will raise to life the dead, by the permission of God; (this he repeated to deny his divinity: and he raised to life 'Ariz (Lazarus) a friend of his; and a son of the old woman, and the daughter of the publican; and they lived, and children were born to them; and Shem the son of Noah, who died immediately); and I will tell you what ye eat and what ye store up in your houses. Verily therein will be a sign unto you, if ye be believers. And I have come unto you as a verifier of that which was before me, of the Law, and to make lawful unto you part of what was made unlawful to you therein; (and he made lawful to them, of fish and fowls, whatsoever is without fin or spur; and it is said that he made lawful all, and that 'part' is used in the sense of 'the whole'): and I have come unto you with a sign from your Lord; therefore fear ye God, and obey me in that which I command you, as to the confession of the unity of God and the service of Him. Verily God is my Lord and your Lord; therefore worship Him. This is the right way. But they accused him of falsehood and believed not in him. And when Jesus perceived their unbelief, he said, Who will be my helpers for God? The apostles answered, We will be the helpers of God. We have believed in God; and bear thou witness, O Jesus, that we are Moslems or resigned. O our Lord, we have believed in that which Thou hast sent down of the Gospel, and we have followed the Apostle Jesus; therefore write us down among those who bear witness of Thy unity and of the truth of Thine apostle. — And the unbelievers among the children of Israel devised a stratagem against Jesus, to slay him treacherously; but God devised a stratagem against them; for He put the likeness of Jesus upon one who intended his slaughter, and they slew him; and Jesus was taken up into heaven, and God is the best of those who devise stratagems. It is related that God sent a cloud to Jesus, and it took him up; but his mother clung unto him and wept: whereupon he said unto her, Verily the resurrection will unite us. — It is also related that he will descend shortly before the resurrection

and judge according to the law of our prophet Mohammed, slay Antichrist and the swine, break the cross, and impose the capitation-tax on unbelievers. — Also, that he will remain, according to one tradition, seven years; according to another, forty years; and die, and be prayed over: but it is probable that by the latter period is meant the whole time of his tarrying upon the earth, before the ascension and after.   [iii, L]

Remember when the apostle said, O Jesus, son of Mary, is thy Lord able to to cause a table to descend unto us from heaven? He replied, Fear God, in demanding signs, if ye be believers. They said, We desire that we may eat therefrom, and that our hearts may be at ease in consequence of additional evidence, and we may know, with increased knowledge, that thou hast spoken truth unto us in asserting thyself to be a prophet, and may be witnesses thereof. — Jesus the son of Mary said, O God, our Lord, cause a table to descend unto us from heaven, that the day of its descent may be unto us a festival, unto the first of us and the last of us (or those who shall come after us), and a sign from Thee of Thy power, and of my prophetic office; and provide us with food thereby; for Thou art the best of providers. — God said, in reply to him, Verily I will cause it to descend unto you; but whosoever of you shall disbelieve after its descent, I will surely punish him with a punishment wherewith I will not punish any other of the peoples. — And the angels descended with it from heaven: upon it were seven cakes of bread and seven fishes; and they ate of them until they were satisfied. And in a tradition related by Ibn-'Abbas it is said that the table brought down from heaven bread and flesh, and they were commanded not to act deceitfully, nor to store up for the morrow; but that some of the people did so, and were transformed into apes and swine.   [v, L]

Propound unto them, as an example, the inhabitants of the city of Antioch, when the apostles of Jesus came unto it; when We sent unto them two, and they charged them with false-hood, wherefore We strengthened them with a third; and they said, Verily we are sent unto you. They replied, Ye are not aught save men like us, and the Compassionate hath not revealed anything: ye do nothing but lie. They said, Our Lord knoweth that we are indeed sent unto you; and naught is imposed on us but the delivering of a plain message, shown to be true by manifest proofs, namely the cure of him who hath been born blind and of the leper and the sick, and the raising of the dead. The people of Antioch said, Verily we presage evil from you; for the rain is withheld from us on your account: if ye desist not, we will assuredly stone you, and a painful punishment shall surely betide you from us. The apostles replied, Your evil luck is with you because of your unbelief. If ye have been warned, will ye presage evil and disbelieve? Nay, ye are an exorbitant people.

And there came from the furthest part of the city a man, Habeeb the carpenter, who had believed in the apostles, running: he said, O my people, follow the apostles: follow those who ask not of you a recompense, and who are rightly directed. And it was said unto him, Art thou of their religion? He replied, And why should I not worship Him who hath created me, and unto whom ye shall be brought back after death? Shall I take deities beside Him? If the Compassionate be pleased to afflict me, their intercession will not avert from me aught, nor will they deliver. Verily, in that case (if I worshiped aught but God), I should be in a manifest error. Verily I believe in your Lord; therefore hear ye me. —But they stoned him, and he died; and it was said unto him at his death, Enter thou into Paradise. And it is said that he entered it alive. He said, O would that my people knew my Lord's forgiveness of me and His having made me one of those who are honored — And We sent not down against his people after his death an army of angels from heaven to destroy them, nor were We sending down angels to destroy any one. Their punishment was naught but one cry which Gabriel uttered against them; and lo, they were extinct. [xxxvi, L]

168

We have cursed the Jews from their disbelief in Jesus and their uttering against Mary a great calumny and their saying, We have killed the Messiah, Jesus the son of Mary, the apostle of God, — Yet they killed him not nor crucified him; but the person whom they crucified was made to appear to them like Jesus; and verily those who disagreed respecting him were in doubt concerning him, or his slaughter; for some of them said, when they saw the slain person, The face is the face of Jesus; but the body is not his body: — and others said, It is he: — they had not knowledge of him; but only followed an opinion. And they did not really kill him; but God took him up unto Himself; and God is mighty and wise. And there is not of the people of the Scripture one but he shall assuredly believe in Jesus before his own death, or before the death of Jesus, when he descendeth shortly before the resurrection; and on the day of resurrection Jesus shall be a witness against them. [iv, L]

When God shall say, on the day of resurrection, O Jesus, son of Mary, hast thou said unto men, Take me and my mother as two deities, beside God? — Jesus shall answer (after it shall have thundered), Extolled be Thy purity from the imputation of aught that is unsuitable to Thee, as the having a partner, and other things! It is not for me to say that which is not right for me. Had I said it, Thou hadst known it. Thou knowest what is in me; but I know not what is in Thee; for Thou well-knowest things unseen. I said not unto them aught but that which thou commandedst me; namely Worship ye God, my Lord and your Lord; — and I was a watcher over them, commanding them to abstain from what they said, while I remained among them: but since Thou hast taken me to Thyself, Thou hast been the watcher over them, and Thou art the witness of all things. If Thou punish such of them as have continued in unbelief, they are Thy servants and Thou mayest do with them as Thou pleasest; and if Thou forgive such of them as have believed, Thou art the Mighty and Wise. [v, L]

When the son of Mary was proposed as an instance (when the saying of God was revealed, Verily ye and what ye worship beside God shall be fuel of hell — and the polytheists said, We are content for our gods to be with Jesus, for he hath been worshiped beside God), lo, thy people, the polytheists, cried out in joy thereat, and they said, Are our gods better, or is he? We are content for our gods to be with him. — They proposed not the instance unto thee otherwise than as a cause of dispute (knowing that the word 'what' applieth to that which is not endowed with reason; so that it doth not reflect upon Jesus, on whom be peace!): yea, they are a contentious people. Jesus is no other than a servant whom We favored with the gift of prophecy; and We proposed him, by reason of his having come into existence without a father, as an instance of the divine power unto the children of Israel. And if We pleased, We would substitute for you angels to succeed in the earth. And verily Jesus shall be a sign of the last hour: it shall be known by his descending: wherefore doubt not thereof. — And say unto them, Follow ye me in confessing the unity of God: this, which I command you to follow, is a right way. And let not the devil turn you away from the religion of God; for he is unto you a manifest enemy. — And when Jesus came with manifest proofs, with miracles and ordinances, he said, I have come unto you with wisdom, and to explain unto you part of the things concerning which ye disagree: therefore fear ye God, and obey me. Verily God is my Lord and your Lord; wherefore worship ye Him: this is a right way. — But the parties disagreed among themselves respecting Jesus, whether he were God, or the son of God, or the third of three: and woe unto them that transgressed in that which they said respecting Jesus, because of the punishment of an afflicting day! [xliii, L]

Verily the similitude of Jesus in the sight of God is as the similitude of Adam. He created Adam of earth: then He said unto him, Be, — and he was. In like manner he said unto Jesus, Be, without a father, — and he was. This is the truth from thy Lord: therefore be not thou of those who doubt. And whosoever of the Christians argueth with thee respecting him after the knowledge that hath come unto thee concerning him, say, Come ye, let us call our sons and your sons and our wives and your wives, and ourselves and yourselves will assemble: then we will invoke, and will lay the curse of God on those who lie, saying, O God, curse the liar respecting the nature of Jesus! — And the prophet invited a company from Nejran to do so, when they had argued with him respecting Jesus; and they said, Wait until we consider our case: then we will come unto thee. And their counselor said, Ye know his prophetic office, and that no people have execrated a prophet but they have perished. They however quieted the man, and departed, and came unto the prophet. And he had come forth, having with him El-Hasan and El-Hoseyn and Fatimeh and 'Alee; and he said unto them, When I pray, say ye Amen. But they refused to execrate, and made peace with him on the condition of their paying tribute. — Verily this is indeed the true history, and there is no deity but God, and verily God is indeed the Mighty, the Wise.   [iii, L]

O people of the Gospel, exceed not the just bounds in your religion, nor say of God aught but the truth. The Messiah, Jesus the son of Mary, was only the apostle of God, and His Word, which he transmitted unto Mary, and a being possessing a spirit from Him. (He is mentioned in conjunction with God, in order to show him honor, and is not, as ye assert, the son of God, or a God with Him, or the third of three; for the being possessing a spirit is compound, and the Deity must be confessed to be pure from the imputation of composition and the relationship of·a compound being to Him.) Therefore believe in God and His apostles, and say not, There are three gods, God and Jesus and his mother. Abstain from this, and say what will be better for you; that is, assert the unity of God. God is only one god. Extolled be His purity from the imputation of His having a son! To Him belongeth whatsoever is in the heavens and whatsoever is in the earth: and God is a sufficient witness thereof. The Messiah doth not disdain to be a servant unto God, nor do the angels who are admitted near unto Him. [iv, L]

[GOD THE CREATOR]

THE command of God is coming, therefore ask not to hasten it. Glory be to Him, and far High is He above what they join with Him. He causes the messenger-spirits to be sent down with the Spirit by His command, upon whichsoever of His servants He pleases, saying: "Warn ye, surely there is no deity but I, therefore reverence Me."

He has made the heavens and the earth with the truth. Far High is He above what they join. He makes man out of a sperm, then lo! he becomes an open disputant. And there are the cattle which He has made, there is therein for you warm costume, and other benefits, and some of them you use for food. And there is for you in them great glory when you bring them home and when you take them out. And they carry your loads to a town you could not reach except with the lives worn out of you. Surely your Lord is most Loving, Merciful.

And He has made horses, and mules, and asses that you may ride them and as things of beauty, and He goes on making what you know not: and the Middle Path reaches unto God, but there are also some crooked ones; and had He wished He could surely have guided you all.

It is He who sends down water from above for you, there is drink therefrom, and there are trees growing therefrom which you use as pastures. With it He causes to grow for you fields of corn, and olives, and dates, and grapes and all kinds of fruit. Most surely there is in this a sign for a people who think. And He orders for you the night and the day, and the sun and

the moon. And the stars are ordered by His command. Most surely in this there are signs for a people who understand. And He has made what He has broadcasted for you in the earth of different kinds of things. Most surely in this there is a sign for a people who remember.

And it is He who orders the sea as a result of which you have for food fresh meat therefrom, and you seek to take out therefrom ornaments which you wear, and you seest the ships cleaving through it, because that you may seek of His grace and that you may give thanks. And He has placed in the earth mountains, lest it may tilt with you, and rivers and roads that you may be guided. And beacons. And they find guidance by means of the stars.

Is He then who creates like one who cannot create? Do you not remember? And if you count the blessings of God you will not be able to number them, most surely God is Forgiving, Merciful. And God knows what you hide and what you show. And those whom they call upon besides God can make nothing and they themselves are made. Dead are they, not living; And they know not when they are going to be raised up.

Your God is the One God. Then as to those who believe not in the Future, their hearts are strangers to the truth and they are big with pride. There is no doubt that God knows what you hide and what you show; surely He loves not the proud. And when it is said to them: "What has your Lord sent down?" they reply: "Stories of the ancients." This is in order that they may bear their own full burdens on the day of the Awakening, and out of the burdens of those whom they have caused to be lost without having any knowledge. Is it not a fact that evil is what they bear?

Surely those before them made their plans, then God brought down their buildings from their foundations, then their roofs fell upon them from above them, and He brought down agony upon them whence they knew not. Then on the day of

the Awakening He will put them to shame, and He will say: "Where are My partners with regard to whom you used to be so perverse?" They who have been given the knowledge will say: "Surely this day shame and evil be upon the disbelievers": — those whom the messenger-spirits give their full reward whilst they are unjust to themselves. Then they will offer submission, saying: "We were not doing evil." "Nay, surely God knows well what you used to do. Therefore enter ye the gates of hell abiding therein. Therefore surely evil is the resting-place of those who are proud." [xvi, s]

175

[THE PARAPETS]

HE says: "Get out of this, dishonored, driven away. Surely, as to him who follows thee from them, I will certainly fill hell with you all together." "And O man! abide thou and thy mate in the garden, then eat ye two wherever you wish, but approach not this tree, otherwise you will become of those who are unjust."

Then the evil-one makes suggestions to them both so as to disclose to them what is hidden from them of their evil nature and says: "Your Lord has not forbidden you eating from this tree except that you may become like two messenger-spirits, or you become immortals." And he swears to them both, "Surely, I am to you of those who are sure advisers."

Then he makes them fall through delusion; then when they both taste this tree, their evil natures are disclosed to them and they begin to cover themselves with the leaves of the garden. And their Lord calls out to them both: "Have I not forbidden you both from this tree, and have I not said to you both that the evil-one is an enemy to you clear?" They say: "Our Lord! We have done injustice to our souls; and if Thou forgive us not and show not mercy to us we shall surely become of those who lose."

He says: "Get down, some of you are, indeed, enemies of others, and for you is a resting-place on this earth and an enjoyment for a time." He says: "In this earth you shall live, and in it you shall die and from it you shall be brought forth."

Ye children of man! We have certainly sent down upon you a dress that covers your evil natures, and an ornament; and the clothing of reverence! that is the best. This is one of God's signs that they may remember. Ye children of man! Let not the evil-one mislead you as he expelled your parents from the garden state of peace, plucking away their dress from them both, in order to disclose to them their evil natures; surely he and his tribe see you whence you see them not: surely, We have made the evil-ones to be the allies of those who believe not.

And when they commit an indecency, they say: "We found our forefathers doing this and God has commanded us to do so." Say: "Surely, God commands not acts of indecency, do you allege against God what you know not?"

Say: "My Lord commands equity, and that you keep your whole beings straight at all times of prayer, and that you call upon Him exclusively doing Him obedience." As He made you first, so will you come round again. A party has He guided, and against another party has He adjudged error as their due. Surely, they have taken the evil-ones as their allies instead of God and they think they are guided. Ye children of man! Put on your beautiful things at the time of each prayer, and eat and drink. But waste not, for He loves not the wasteful.

Say: "Who has forbidden the beautiful things of God which He has produced for His servants and the pure foods?" Say: "These are for the faithful in the life of this world, and exclusively theirs on the day of the Awakening." In this way do We explain Our signs for a people who know.

Say: "This is it that my Lord has forbidden: indecencies which are apparent and which are hidden, and sin, and revolting without just cause, and that you join with God that for which

He has sent down no warrant, and that you say against God what you know not."

And for every people there is a term, so that when their term arrives they cannot remain behind for an hour nor can they precede it. Ye children of Man! When My messengers come to you from amongst you relating My signs to you, then as to him who is reverent and does good there is then no fear on such, nor shall they grieve. And as to those who belie My signs and are filled with pride turning away therefrom, these are the companions of the fire, in it they abide.

Then who is more unjust than he who forges a lie against God, or belies His signs? These are the people who will receive their share of what is written down. When our messengers will come to them, they will give them their full reward. They will say: "Where is that which you called upon besides God?" They will reply: "Lost are they from us." And they will bear witness against themselves that they were disbelievers. He will say: "Join ye the peoples who have gone before you from among the jinn and men into the fire." Every time a people enters it, it will disapprove of its predecessor until they have caught it up all together; those who have come behind will say with regard to those who have gone before: "Our Lord! They caused us to be lost, then give them double the agony of the fire." He will say: "For each of you is double but you know it not." And those who have gone before will say to those who have come behind: "There is no distinction granted you over us, then taste the agony for what you did."

As to those who belie our signs and turn away from them in pride, the doors of heaven shall not be opened for them nor shall they enter the garden until a cable enter the eye of a needle. And it is thus that We reward the guilty. Hell shall be a cradle and a covering to them, and it is thus that We reward the unjust.

And there are those who believe and do good deeds — and We are not burdening any soul except according to its capacity —

these are the companions of the garden, in it they abide. And
We will take away from their breasts all kinds of envy, rivers
flowing underneath them and they will say: "All praise belongs to God who has guided us to this state and we were not
able to guide ourselves if God had not guided us, most certainly the messengers of our Lord came to us with the truth."
And a voice will call out to them: "This is the garden which
you have inherited on account of what you did."

And the companions of the garden will call out to the companions of the fire saying: "We have indeed found what was
held out to us by our Lord to be the truth, then have you
found what was held out to you by your Lord to be the truth?"
They will reply: "Yes." And a caller between them will call
out, "The disapproval of God be upon the unjust, who kept
away from God's way and sought to make it crooked and who
did not believe in the Future."

And between the two, the garden and the fire, there shall be a
barrier, and upon the parapets there shall be men who will
recognize all by their expressions. And they shall call out to
the companions of the garden saying: "Peace be upon you."
And these will not have entered therein but will be hoping
to do so. But when their eyes are turned towards, and meet,
those who are the companions of the fire, they will say: "Our
Lord! put us not together with the unjust people."

And the companions of the parapets will call out to men whom
they will recognize by their expressions saying: "What use
have been to you your gatherings and your prides? Are these
the people you used to swear would not receive any part of
God's mercy?" And to the others they will say: "Enter ye the
garden, no fear upon you nor will you grieve." And the companions of the fire will call out to the companions of the
garden saying: "Pour down upon us some water or out of
what God has provided you with." They will say: "God has
forbidden these things to the unbelievers; those who took
their religion as a plaything and a vanity, and whom the life

of the nearer world had deluded." So that We have put them away this day as they put away the meeting of this day; and as they used to deny Our signs.

And most surely We have brought them a Book which We have explained with a basis of knowledge and which is a guidance and a mercy to the people who believe. Do they wait for aught but the end thereof? The day when the end thereof comes, those who had put it aside before will say: "Surely the messengers of our Lord came to us with the truth. Then are there for us any seconders so that they may do something for us, or that we may be sent back so that we may do otherwise than what we used to do?" Surely they have lost their souls and lost from them is what they used to forge. [vii, s]

Surely your Lord is God who has made the heavens and the earth into six periods and still remains firm upon His throne; He causes the night to cover the day, each pursuing the other incessantly. And He has made the sun, and the moon and the stars, all obedient to His command. Are not the making and the command His? Blessed is God, Lord of all the worlds.

Call upon your Lord with humility and in private. Surely He loves not the transgressors. And do not do evil in the earth after the reformation thereof, and call upon Him with fear and with hope. Surely the mercy of God is near to those who do good.

And it is He who sends the breezes bearing good news of His mercies to come. Until they bear heavy clouds which We drive to a dead soil then We send down water thereon, then We cause to grow up by means of that water every kind of fruit. In this way shall We cause the dead to come out, that you may remember. And a good soil brings forth its vegetation with the command of its Lord. And a bad soil brings forth nothing but unhappiness. In this way do We illustrate our signs in various ways for a people who give thanks. [vii, s]

[THE CATTLE]

SURELY God causes the seed and the stone to sprout; he brings forth the living from the dead, and He is the Bringer forth of the dead from the living. This is God, where then are you turned to? He is the Opener forth of the morns, and He makes the night as a means of rest, and the sun and the moon as a means of reckoning: this is the determination of all-Might, all-Knowing. And it is He who has made the stars for you that you may be guided by them in the glooms of the land and the sea; We have certainly explained Our signs for a people who know. And it is He who has evolved you from a single being, then there is a place for you to seek rest and a place to go back to. Surely We have explained Our signs for a people who understand. And it is He who sends down water from above, then We bring forth therewith growths of all kinds, then We bring forth therefrom green foliage from which We bring forth grains piled up; and out of the sheaths of palms are clusters of fruits hanging down; and gardens of grapes, and olives, and pomegranates, similar and dissimilar. Look ye towards its fruit when it fructifies, and the ripening thereof. Surely, in this are signs for a people who believe. And they have made for God associates of the jinn and He made them; and they have devised for Him sons and daughters, without any knowledge. Glory be to Him, and far above is He from that which they attribute to Him.

Originator of the heavens and the earth. How could there be to Him a child? Nor is there to Him any female companion, and He made all things, and all things He knows.

This is God, your Lord, there is no deity but He, maker of all things; then serve Him, for He is Controller over all things. Eyes cannot comprehend Him and He comprehends all eyes; and He is all-Subtle, all-Aware. Surely there has come to you enlightenment from your Lord, then he who is enlightened is so for His own soul, and he who remains blind is so against his own soul.

And it is He who evolved gardens trellised and untrellised; and the date-palms; and fields with the various produce thereof; and olives; and pomegranates, similar and dissimilar. Eat ye of the fruit thereof when they yield fruit; and give its stated due on the day of its reaping; and waste not; surely He loves not those who waste. And of the cattle, some are for carrying loads and some are too low to carry loads; eat ye out of what God has provided you with, and follow not the footsteps of the evil-one. Surely, he is to you an enemy clear.

There are eight males and females: two of the sheep and two of the goat — Say: "Has He forbidden the two males thereof or the two females, or that which is wrapped up in the wombs of the two females? Give me the news with knowledge if ye be truthful." And of the camel two, and two of the cow; say: "Are the two males thereof forbidden or the two females, or what is wrapped up in the wombs of the two females? or were you witnesses when God ordered you this? Who is more unjust then than one who forges a lie against God, that he may without any knowledge cause mankind to be lost? Surely, God does not guide the unjust people.

Say: "I find not, in what has been revealed to me, anything forbidden to a person wishing to take a meal except it be: — a dead body, or flowing blood, or the flesh of the swine, for that is impure; or what is disobedience, being slaughtered in the name of other than God; but whoever is compelled to it, without being rebellious, neither going beyond the limit, then surely thy Lord is Forgiving, Merciful."

And the Jews We forbade every animal with hoofs; and of the cow and goat We forbade them their fat except what was wrapped up in their backs or their bowels or what was attached to their bones. Thus did We reward them for their rebellion, and We are surely the Truthful.

182

And this Koran is a blessed Book which We have sent down; follow ye it, then, and be reverent, that ye may be shown mercy. Lest you should say: "The Book had only been sent down to two classes before us, and we were unaware of their readings." Or lest you should say: "Had a Book been sent down upon us We would certainly have been better guided than they." Now, certainly, clear evidence has come to you from your Lord and a guidance and a mercy. Who is then more unjust than he who belies the signs of God and keeps away from them? We will reward those who keep away from Our signs with an evil agony on account of their having done so. What do they expect, except the coming to them of the messenger-spirits, or the coming of thy Lord, or the coming of some of the signs of thy Lord? The day some of the signs of thy Lord come to appear, its believing will not profit any soul that did not believe before, or which having believed earned no good. Say: "Wait, we too are waiting."

As to those who have split up their religion and become sects, thou O Mohammed! hast nothing in common with them. Their affair is towards God, He will thereafter inform them as to what they used to do. He who brings one good, for him thereafter there are ten like thereof; and he who brings an evil will not be rewarded except with its like, and they will not be wronged.

Say: "As to me, my Lord has guided me to the Right Path: an upright faith, the religion of Abraham the single-minded, and he was not of the pagans." Say: "Surely, my prayer and my sacrifice and my living and my dying are all for the sake of God, Lord of all the worlds; He has no associate, and so am I commanded, and I am the first of the Moslems."

Say: "Shall I seek a lord other than God, and He is the Lord of all things," and no soul does anything except for itself, and no bearer shall bear the burden of another; then towards your Lord will be your return, so that He will inform you of that in which you used to differ. And it is He who has made you successors of the earth, and He raises some of you above the others in degrees, that He may discipline you concerning that which He has given you. Surely, thy Lord is quick in respect of the consequences, and surely He is indeed Forgiving, Merciful. [vi, s]

THE THUNDER

A. L. M. R. THESE are the Signs of the Book! and that which was sent down to thee from thy Lord is the truth: but most men do not believe. It is God who raised the heavens without pillars that ye can see; then ascended the Throne, and subdued the sun and the moon: each runneth to its appointed goal, to rule every thing, to manifest signs. Haply ye will be convinced of meeting your Lord! And it is He who spread out the earth, and put thereon firm mountains, and rivers; and of every fruit He hath made therein two kinds: He maketh the night to cover the day; verily in that are signs for reflecting folk. And on the earth are neighboring tracts, and gardens of grapes, and corn, and palms clustered and not clustered at the root; they are watered by the same water, yet we make some better than others for food: verily in that are signs for folk that have wits.

If ever thou dost wonder, wonderful is their saying, "What! when we have become dust, shall we indeed become a new creation?" These are they who disbelieve in their Lord: and these shall have the shackles on their necks, and these shall be the inmates of the fire to abide therein for ever. They will bid thee hasten evil rather than good: examples have passed away before them; and verily thy Lord is full of forgiveness unto men despite their iniquity; and verily thy Lord is heavy in punishing. And they who disbelieve say, "Unless a sign be sent down to him from his Lord." —Thou art but a warner, and to every people its guide. God knoweth what every woman beareth, and the decrease of the wombs and the increase; for the pattern of all things is with Him, who knoweth the hidden and the seen, the Great, the Most High. Equal is he of you who concealeth his words and he that proclaimeth them: he who hideth by night, and he who goeth abroad by day. Each hath angels before him and behind him, who watch over him by God's command. Verily God doth not change towards a people, till they change themselves; and when God willeth evil unto a people, there is no averting it, nor have they any protector beside Him.

It is He who showeth you the lightning for fear and hope of rain, and gathereth the lowering clouds, and the Thunder magnifieth His praise, and the angels, for awe of Him, and He sendeth His thunderbolts and smiteth therewith whom He pleaseth: — and they are wrangling about God! but strong is His might! Unto Him is the true cry: but those whom they cry to beside Him shall answer them naught save as one who stretcheth forth his hands to the water that it may reach his mouth, but it doth not reach it! The cry of the unbelievers is but in error. And unto God bow down all things in the heavens and the earth, willingly or unwillingly, and their shadows at morn and eve!

Say: Who is Lord of the heavens and the earth? Say: God. Say: Why then have ye taken beside Him Patrons who are powerless for weal or woe to themselves? Say: What! are the blind and the seeing alike? or are darkness and light the same? or have they made Partners for God, who create as He creates, so that they confuse the creation? Say: God is the Creator of all things, He is the One, the Conqueror. He sendeth down water from heaven; and the valleys flow in their degree, and the torrent beareth along foaming froth, and from the ore which they burn in the fire, desiring ornament or necessaries, a scum like it ariseth. So doth God liken truth and falsehood. As to the scum it passeth off as refuse, and what profiteth man it remaineth on the earth. Thus doth God frame parables.

For those who respond to their Lord, good; but those who respond not to Him, had they all that the earth containeth and its like beside it, they would surely give it in ransom: these shall have an evil reckoning, and Hell shall be their home, — and wretched the bed! Is he who knoweth that what hath been sent down to thee from thy Lord is naught but the truth, like to him who is blind? but men of understanding alone will mind, who fulfill their covenant with God and break not the compact; and who join what God hath bidden to be joined, and who fear their Lord and dread the evil reckoning; and who are patient, seeking the face of their Lord, and perform prayer and give alms secretly and openly of what we have provided them, and turn away evil with good: for these are the reward of the Abode, — gardens of eternity, which they shall enter together with those who were just to their fathers and their wives and their offspring: and the angels shall go in unto them at every gate saying: — "Peace be upon you! because ye were patient." And pleasant is the reward of the Abode! But those who break God's covenant after they have pledged it, and cut asunder what God hath bidden to be joined, and work iniquity in the earth, for these is a curse and a sore abode!

God is lavish with provision to whom He pleaseth, or He stinteth it. And they rejoice in the life of this world; but the life of this world is but a passing joy to the life to come. And they who disbelieve say, "Unless a sign be sent down to him from his Lord —" Say: God truly misleadeth whom He will; and He guideth to himself those who repent, who believe, and whose hearts are at peace in the remembrance of God! yea, in the remembrance of God shall the hearts be at peace of those who believe and do the things that are right — good betide them, and happy be their goal! Thus have we sent thee among a nation, before whom other nations have passed away, that thou mayest tell them what we have inspired thee with: yet they disbelieve in the Merciful! Say: He is my Lord — there

is no God but Him. In Him do I put my trust, and unto Him is my return. Though there were a Koran by which the mountains were removed or the earth cloven or the dead given speech — Nay! to God belongeth the rule in all: know not they who believe, that if God pleased, He would certainly have guided men in all?

And calamity shall not cease to befall the unbelievers for what they have done, or settle hard by their dwellings, until the promise of God shall come to pass. Verily God will not fail in what He promised.

Before thee apostles have been mocked at — and long I suffered those who disbelieved; then I took hold of them; and how great was my punishment! Who then is he that is standing over every soul to mark what it hath earned? Yet they made Partners with God! Say: Name them! could ye inform him of what He knoweth not in the earth, or are they aught beyond words? Nay, their artifice commended itself to those who disbelieve; and they are turned aside from the road; and whom God misleadeth, he hath no guide. Torment is theirs in the life of this world, and assuredly the torment of the world to come shall be worse, and they shall have no one to ward them from God.

A likeness of the Paradise which is promised to those that fear God: — the rivers flow beneath it; its food and its shades are everlasting. That is the end of those who fear God: but the end of the unbelievers is the Fire.

They to whom we have given the Book rejoice in what hath been sent down to thee, yet some of the confederates deny a part of it. Say: I am commanded only to worship God, and not to associate any with Him: on Him I cry, and unto Him is my goal. Thus have we sent down the Koran as an Arabic judgment; and assuredly, if thou followed their desires after the knowledge had come to thee, thou shouldst have no protector nor warder against God. And we have sent apostles before thee, and gave them wives and offspring. But to no apostle was it given to bring a sign save by God's permission: to each age its Book. God wipeth out or confirmeth what He pleaseth, and with Him is the Mother of the Book. And whether we show thee somewhat of that which we promised them, or take thee hence before; verily, it is thine to announce only, and ours to take account. See they not that we come into the land and cut down its chiefs? And when God judgeth, there is none to reverse. His sentence: and He is swift to reckon. And those who were before them plotted: but God's is the master plot: He knoweth what every one soul earneth, and the infidels shall know for whom is the reward of the abode.

And those who disbelieve shall say, "Thou art not sent from God." Say: God is witness enough between me and you, and he that hath knowledge of the Book. [xiii, P]

THE PERIOD OF HARANGUE

A.D. 622-632

[THE LAWS]

O YE men! Eat of the produce of the earth things that are lawful and pure, and follow not the footsteps of the evil-one; surely, he is an enemy to you clear. All he does is to bid you to evil, and to things obscene, and that you say against God what you know not. And when it is said to them, "Follow that which God has sent down," they say, "Rather, we will follow that upon which we found our forefathers." What! even if their forefathers had no sense at all, and they were not guided aright?

And the case of those who have chosen disbelief is like this: — there is one who shouts to someone who hears not but a mere cry and a sound. They are deaf, dumb, blind, so that they have no sense.

O ye who believe! Eat of the good things that We have provided you with, and give thanks to God, if Him alone you serve. All He has forbidden you is the dead, and the blood, and the flesh of swine, and that over which any other name than that of God has been used, but if anyone is constrained without wishing to be disobedient, nor going beyond the limit, no sin be upon such. For God is Forgiving, Merciful.

Surely those who conceal that which God has sent down of the Book and sell it for a mean price, these devour not but fire into their insides; and God will not speak to them on the day of the Awakening, nor will He purify them and for them is a painful agony. These are the people who have bought error for guidance, and agony for pardon. Then, what fortitude is theirs in the fire! This is so, because God has caused this Book to be sent down with the truth; and those who differ with regard to this Book are in a far-off obstinacy.

There is no virtue in your turning your faces towards the East or the West, but virtuous is he who believes in God, and in the Future day, and in the messenger-spirits, and the Book, and the prophets; and who gives his wealth, in spite of his love for it, to the near of kin, and the orphans, and the needy, and the wayfarer, and the beggars, and in ransoming the slaves; and who keeps up the prayers, and pays the stated alms; and those who fulfill their covenants when they covenant; and the persevering ones in hardship, and injury, and in time of war: these are the truthful, and these! they are the reverent.

O ye who believe! An equal compensation is prescribed for you in the matter of the slain; the free man for the free man, and the slave for the slave, and the female for the female. But as to him who is remitted something by his brother, he should follow the remission with fairness and payment of compensation to him the aggrieved with kindness. This is a relaxation from your Lord and a mercy. But if anyone exceeds the limit after this, there is for him then a painful agony.

And for you, in this law of equal compensation, O men of understanding! There is the preservation of life, and that you may be reverent. It is prescribed for you that when one of you is face to face with death, and if he leave any goods, that he make a legacy in favor of the parents, and the kindred, with fairness: a duty incumbent on the reverent. He, then, who changes it after having heard it, the sin thereof then is on those alone who change it: surely God is Hearing, Knowing. But if anyone fears partiality, or sin on the part of the legator, then, it is no sin upon him if he make peace between the parties: surely God is Forgiving, Merciful.

O ye who believe! Fasting is prescribed for you, as it was prescribed for those who preceded you — that you may be reverent: for a certain number of days. Then for anyone of you who is sick, or on journey, there is then the same number of other days. And for those who find it hard to bear, there is redemption by feeding the poor — but he who does good of his own accord, then it is better for him. And if you fast, it would be better for you, if you knew.

The month of Ramadan is one in which was sent down the Koran, a guidance for mankind, and clear proofs of guidance, and the discrimination. Then let him amongst you who is present in this month fast therein. And if one be sick, or on journey, then there is an equal number of other days. God wishes you ease, and He does not wish you discomfort, and that you may complete the required number of fasts, and that you may declare the greatness of God, for His having guided you; and that you may give thanks. And when My servants ask thee about Me, "Lo! I AM SURELY NEAR." I respond to the call of the caller when he calls Me. Then should they respond to Me, and believe in Me, that they may proceed aright.

On the night of the fast, it is lawful for you to approach your wives; they are a garment for you, and you are a garment for them. God knows that you have been lessening your rights, so He has turned to you and freed you from disability; now, then, enjoy their company, and seek that which God has prescribed for you, and eat and drink till is manifested to you the white thread of the light of the morn from the black thread of darkness. Then complete the fast till night, and keep away from them your wives while you pass the time in the mosques.

These be the bounds of God, therefore come not near to transgress them; thus does God make clear His signs to men that they may be reverent. And do not swallow up your wealth among yourselves improperly, and make not presents of it to the authorities, that you may sinfully devour the wealth of other men the while you know.

They ask thee about the new moons; say, "They are times appointed for the use of men, and for pilgrimage." And there is no virtue in your going to your houses by the backs thereof, but virtue consists in being reverent; then enter your houses by their doors, and reverence God, that you may prosper. And fight in the way of God those who fight you, but exceed not the limit: for God loves not those who exceed the limit. And kill them where you find them, and turn them out from whence they have turned you out, for persecution in faith is worse than war. And war not with them near the sacred mosque, unless they war with you therein; but if they fight you, then fight them. Such is the reward of the disbelievers.

But if they desist, then surely God is Forgiving, Merciful. And fight them until there be no persecution and the judgment be God's. But if they desist, then let there be no hostilities save against the unjust.

One sacred month for another sacred month, and the law of equal recompense applies to all sacred things. Then if anyone takes the aggressive against you, take the aggressive against

him, just as he has taken the aggressive against you; and reverence God, and know that God is with the reverent.

And spend in the way of God, but throw not yourselves into ruin with your own hands; and do good, for God loves the doers of good. And carry out the pilgrimage, and the visit to Kaabah for the sake of God. But if you are intercepted, then send whatever sacrificial offering you can afford, and shave not your heads until the offering reaches its destination; but if one of you be sick, or is suffering from injury in the head, he should compensate the shaving of the head by fasting, or almsgiving, or sacrificing; but when you are safe, then anyone taking advantage of the pilgrimage and the visit at one and the same time should offer such sacrifice as he can afford. And if one cannot, then three days' fasting in the period of the Haj, and seven days when you return home: these make the ten complete days. This is for him whose family is not resident near the sacred mosque. And reverence God, and know that God is severe in respect of the consequences.

Pilgrimage takes place in the well-known months; whoever, then, undertakes the pilgrimage during those months, there is to be no intercourse with women, nor the commission of any sins, nor any wrangling, during the period of the Haj. And whatever good you do, God knows it all. And make provision for the journey, because the good of making provision consists in being reverent. And reverence Me, O ye who are possessed of understanding.

There is no blame on you that you seek increase from your Lord. But when you disperse from Arafat, then remember God near the holy monument Mubdalafa and remember Him as He has directed you; and before this you were of those who are lost. Then disperse again from whence men disperse, and ask forgiveness of God. Surely God is Forgiving, Merciful.

Then when you have completed your devotions of pilgrimage remember God as your remembering of your forefathers, or

rather a stronger remembering. Then there are some who say, "Our Lord! give us good in this world," and they have no share in the Future. And there are some of them who say, "Our Lord! give us good in this world, and good in the Future, and save us from the agony of the fire." These are the people for whom there is a share out of what they have earned: and God is quick in counting.

And remember God during a certain number of days. Then whoever hastens during the course of two days there is no sin upon him, and whoever remains behind there is no sin upon him either — for him who is reverent. And reverence God, and know that you are to be gathered towards Him.

And there is someone amongst men whose speech about the life of this world causes thee to wonder, and he calls God to witness that which is in his heart, and he is most violent in disputations. And when he turns back he strives in the land in order to cause disorder therein and to destroy the fields and the flocks: and God loves not disorder. And when it is said to him "Reverence God" his pride carries him on to his sin, then sufficient to him is hell, and surely an evil cradle is that.

And amongst men there be one who offers his soul, seeking its acceptance by God: for God is Loving towards His servants. O ye who believe! Enter into the Peace (Islam) all together, and follow not the footsteps of the evil-one; he is surely to you a clear enemy. But if you slip after what has come to you of the clear signs, then know that God is Mighty, Knowing. They wait not but that God should come to them in the shadows of the clouds, as well as the messenger-spirits, and the affair be settled: and to God is the return of all affairs.

Ask the children of Israel, how many clear signs did We give them? and whoever changes the blessing of God after it has come to him, then surely God is severe in respect of the consequences. Fair seems the life of this world to those who have chosen disbelief, and they mock at those who believe; and those who practice reverence shall be above them on the day of the Awakening. And God makes provision for whom He pleases without measure.

All mankind are a single community, then God sends His prophets, bearers of glad tidings and as warners; and He sends with them the Book with the truth that He may decide between mankind concerning that in which they differ; and none differ therein save those to whom the book has been given after clear signs have come to them, out of hostility amongst themselves. Then God directs aright those who believe, in respect of that in which they differ about the truth, with His own authority. For God guides whom He pleases to the Right Path.

Do you reckon that you will enter the garden without undergoing the like of that which happened to those who preceded you? Distress befell them, and affliction, and they were shaken till the messenger and those who had believed with him said, "When will come the help of God?" Is it not a fact that the help of God is nigh?

They ask thee, as to what they may spend. Say, "Whatever goods you spend, they are for the parents, and the kindred, and the orphans, and the needy, and the wayfarer, and whatever good you do God knows it all. War has been prescribed for you and that displeases you, it may be you dislike something whilst it is good for you; and it may be that you love something and that is bad for you, because God knows it, and you know it not.

They ask thee concerning the holy month — as to fighting therein. Say, "Fighting therein is a serious matter." But hindering men from God's way, and disbelieving in Him, and hindering them from the holy mosque, and turning out its people therefrom are more serious with God; and persecution in faith is more serious than war. And they will not cease fighting with you till they turn you back from your faith if they can. And if anyone of you turns back from his faith, then dies whilst he is a disbeliever; these, then, are people whose deeds

go for nothing, in this world and in the Future. And these are the companions of the Fire, in it they abide. As to those who have believed, and those who have fled their homes, and struggled hard in God's way, these do hope for God's mercy: for God is Forgiving, Merciful.

They ask thee about intoxicants and games of chance. Say, "In both these there is great sin, and some gain for men, and the sin thereof is more serious than the gain thereof." And they ask thee as to what they should spend. Say, "What you can spare." Thus does God make clear to you His signs — that you may think — concerning this world and the future.

And they ask thee about the orphans. Say, "To do good to them is best." And if you share things with them, they be your brethren. And God knows the evil doer from the right doer. And if God had willed He would certainly have made matters difficult for you. Surely God is Mighty, Wise.

And ye believing men! marry not pagan women till they believe, and a believing maid is better than a pagan woman although you fancy her; and ye believing women! marry not pagan men till they believe, and a believing servant is better than a pagan free man though you fancy him. These call you to the fire, but God calls you to the garden and the forgiveness with His own authority. And He makes clear His signs for men that they may be mindful.

And they ask thee about the menses. Say, "It is a minor hurt." Then avoid women during the menses, and approach them not till they are in a state of purity, but when they are in a state of purity you may come to them whence God has ordered you. Surely God loves those who turn towards Him, and He loves the pure. Your wives are a tilth for you, then come to your tilth as you please, and send forward good for your souls; and reverence God, and know that you are going to meet Him. And give glad tidings to the believers.

And make not use of God's name in swearing, as an excuse for not doing good and being reverent, and making peace between men: for God is Hearing, Knowing. God will not call you to account for oaths taken casually, but He will call you to account for what your hearts have earned. For God is Forgiving, Forbearing.

Those who swear off from their wives, they have to wait four months, then if they go back, surely God is Forgiving, Merciful. And if they have resolved on divorce, then also God is surely Hearing, Knowing. And the divorced women must wait for three courses; and it is not lawful for them to conceal What God has formed in their wombs, if they believe in God and the Future day. And their husbands have a right to take them back during this period, if they desire to make peace. And the wives have a right against their husbands just as there is a right against them with fairness. And the men are a degree above the women. For God is Mighty, Wise.

Divorce may be pronounced twice, then there should be keeping with fairness or leaving with goodness. And it is not lawful for you to take back anything out of what you have given them, unless they two fear that they will not be able to keep within the bounds of God. But if you fear that they two will not be able to keep within the bounds of God, there is no blame on them two in what she gives up to be free. These be the bounds of God, therefore, exceed not the limits; and whoever exceeds the bounds of God, these, then, are the people who are unjust.

But if he finally divorces her then she is not lawful for him until after she has married another husband; but if he also divorce her then there is no blame on them both if they return to each other, provided they think that they can keep within the bounds of God. And these are the bounds of God which He makes clear to a people who know. And when you divorce your wives so that they complete their term, then keep them with fairness or leave them with fairness. And detain them not to cause injury resulting in your exceeding the limit; and whoever does that, he has indeed done injustice to himself.

And do not make a mockery of the commandments of God, and keep in mind the favor of God upon you, and what He has sent down upon you of the Book, and the wisdom, with which He admonishes you. And reverence God and know that God knows everything.

And when you have divorced your wives and they have completed their term of waiting then hinder them not from marrying their husbands when they have agreed amongst themselves with fairness: thus does He admonish him who amongst you believes in God and the Future day; this is cleaner for you and purer. God knows and you know not.

And mothers should suckle their children for two complete years, in the case of those who wish to complete their period of suckling. And it is the duty of the father of the child to feed them and clothe them with fairness. No soul is burdened but to the extent of its capacity; let not the mother suffer injury on account of her child; nor the father on account of his child; and a similar law holds for his heir; but if they both desire to wean the child by mutual consent and counsel, then there is no blame on them either. And if you men desire to provide a wet nurse for your children, then there is no blame on you when you pay what you agree to pay with fairness; and reverence God, and know that God sees what you do.

And as for those of you who die and leave wives behind, they should keep themselves in waiting for four months and ten days, then when they have completed their term, there is no blame on you in what they do with themselves in a fair way; for God is aware of what you do.

And there is no blame on you in respect of your offer of marriage to such women that you convey it secretly, or keep it concealed in your minds; God knows that you will remember them, but make no proposal to them in secret. Save you speak a fair speech, and resolve not on the marriage tie until the prescribed term is completed; and know that God knows what is in your minds, therefore, beware of Him: and know that God is Forgiving, Forbearing.

There is no blame on you if you divorce your wives whom you have not touched, or for whom you have not fixed a portion; and make provision for them, the well-to-do according to his means and the straitened in circumstances according to his means, a provision with fairness; a duty incumbent on all doers of good. And if you divorce them before you have touched them, but you have appointed for them a certain portion, then pay half of what you have appointed unless they remit, or he remits in whose hand is the marriage tie; and if you remit, it is nearer to reverence; and forget not benevolence amongst yourselves; for God sees what you do.

Be careful as to prayers, especially the most excellent prayer, and stand up for the sake of God in a devout manner. But if you are in danger then say your prayers on foot, or whilst riding, but when you are safe, then remember God as He has taught you what you did not know before.

And as to those of you who die and leave wives behind, there should be a legacy for their wives for a year's maintenance without their being turned out; but if they themselves go away, there is no blame on you with regard to what they do concerning themselves in a fair manner; for God is Mighty, Wise. And for the divorced women also there is to be provision with fairness; a duty incumbent on the reverent. In this way does God make clear to you His signs that you may understand.

The attribute of those who spend their wealth in God's way is like the attribute of a grain which grows into seven ears, in each ear a hundred grains: and God multiplies it for whom He pleases: for God is Vast, Knowing. As to those who spend their wealth in God's way, then follow not what they have spent with show of obligation, nor injury, for them is their reward with their Lord, and there is no fear on them nor shall they grieve.

199

Fair speech and forgiveness are better than charity followed by injury. For God is Rich, Forbearing. O Ye who believe! render not void your charity by show of obligation and injury, like him who spends his wealth for the sake of show of mankind, and he does not believe in God and the Future day. His attribute is as the attribute of a smooth rock with some soil thereon, then it catches a heavy rain which then leaves it a bare stone. Nothing which they earned is of any avail. For God guides not the disbelieving people.

The attribute of those who spend their wealth seeking the good will of God, and with firm faith out of their own souls, is like the attribute of a garden on a hill: if it catches heavy rain it brings forth its fruit in double quantity; but if it does not catch heavy rain then dew is sufficient for it; and God sees what you do.

Would any of you desire that he should have a garden of the date-palms and vines, with streams flowing underneath, in which there is for him each kind of fruit, and old age has overtaken him, whilst he has weakly offspring, that then the garden should meet with a storm in which there is fire so that it is burnt up? Like that! does God explain to you the signs that you may think.

O Ye who believe! spend of the good things which you earn, and out of what We produce for you from the earth, and intend not to give thereof what is worthless, and you would not take it yourself save with eyes closed thereat; and know that God is Rich, Praised. The evil-one holds out to you poverty, and bids you niggardliness; and God holds out to you forgiveness from Himself and increase: for God is Vast, Knowing. He grants wisdom to whom He pleases, and whoever is granted wisdom then he is indeed granted a great good. And none remember this except those possessed of understanding.

And whatever you spend in alms, or in vows that you vow, then surely God knows it all. And for the unjust there is none to help. If you disclose your alms, even then it is well done, but if you keep them secret, and give them to the poor, then that is better still for you; and this wipes off from you some of your evil deeds. And God is aware of what you do. Thou art not responsible for their guidance, but God guides whom He pleases. And whatever you spend in doing good it is for your own souls; and spend not aught but to seek the favor of God and whatever you spend in doing good will be fully credited to you; and you shall not be wronged.

Give to the poor who are intercepted in God's way, they have not the means to move about in the land, the stranger thinks them to be rich on account of their abstention, thou canst recognize them by their faces, they do not beg from men obstinately; and whatever you spend in doing good then surely God knows it.

As to those who spend their wealth by night and by day, secretly and openly — therefore for them is their reward with their Lord. And there is no fear on them nor shall they grieve.

As to those who live on usury they stand not except like the standing of one whom the evil-one has confounded with his touch. That is so because they say, "Trade is just like usury," whilst God has allowed trade and forbidden usury. Then whosoever receives this admonition from his Lord, and keeps away from usury, then let what has passed away be his; and his affair is with God. But whoever comes back then these be the companions of the fire, in it they abide. God voids usury and advances charities; and God loves not a single ungrateful sinner.

Surely those who believe and do good deeds, and keep up the prayer, and pay the stated alms, they have their reward with their Lord; and there is no fear upon them, nor shall they grieve. O ye who believe! Reverence God and abandon what remains of usury, if you are believers. But if you do it not, then beware of war on the part of God and His Messenger, but if you turn to God then yours be your capitals; oppress not, and be not oppressed.

But if a person be in straitened circumstances, then give him time till he be in easy circumstances. But if you make a charity of it, it is better for you, if ye knew. And fear the day you shall be made to return therein to God; then each soul shall be paid back in full what it has earned, nor shall they be wronged.

O ye who believe! When you transact a mutual loan transaction up to a fixed term, then write it down. And let the writer betwixt you write it down with justice. And let not the writer refuse to write as God has taught him to write, then let him write it down. And let him upon whom be the liability dictate, and let him reverence his Lord, and let him not depreciate anything therefrom. But if he upon whom be the liability is lacking in understanding, or is infirm, or be incapable of dictating by himself then let his attorney dictate with justice. And two male witnesses amongst you should witness it; but if there be not two males available then let there be a male and two female witnesses out of those you choose, in order that if one of the females be in error, the other of them may be able to remind her. And let not the witnesses refuse to give evidence when they are called, and be not negligent in writing it down whether the loan be small or large to a fixed term. This is more equitable with God, and is better suited to establish evidence, and is more likely to prevent your falling into doubts, except it be a cash transaction which passes from hand to hand amongst yourselves, then there is no blame on you if you write it not. And have witnesses when you trade with one another, and let not the writer or the witness be harmed. And if you do so, then that is a sin in you. And reverence God; and God teaches you; and God knows everything. And if you be on journey, and find not a writer, then let there be a pledge with possession. Then if some of you trust the others, then let the trustee pay back the trust, and let him reverence God, his Lord. And conceal not the evidence, for whoever conceals it, then he is sinful in his heart. And God knows what you do. [ii, s]

O ʏᴇ mankind! Reverence your Lord who made you from a single being, and from that being He made its mate, and from the twain He caused to spread many men and many women; and reverence God by Whom you question one another and pay respect to the ties of relationship. Surely, God watches over you.

And give the orphans their belongings, and change not the worthless for their good things, and consume not their belongings as your own; that indeed is a heinous sin. And if you fear that you will not be able to do justice to the orphan girls by taking them in marriage, then marry whom you like from amongst other women, two at a time, or three, or four; but if you are afraid that even then you will not be able to keep equality amongst your wives, then marry only one, or that which your right hands have possessed: this is nearer to keeping you from doing injustice.

And give women their dowries with good accord; but if they of their own wish like to give up some of it, in your favor, then consume it with ease and pleasure. And do not hand over your belongings which God has made a means of your living to the weak of understanding, but feed them, and clothe them therewith and speak to them a fair speech. And discipline the orphans till they reach the age of marriage, so that if you find them strong in understanding, then give them back their belongings; and consume not their belongings wastefully, and hastily, fearing that they should reach their maturity; and he who is rich should abstain from consuming it, but he who is poor, let him consume of it with fairness: but when you give them back their belongings, then take witness against them; and God is a sufficient Accountant.

For men, there is a share in what their parents and their relatives leave behind, and for women is a share in what their parents and relatives leave behind, be it little, or be it much: a stated

share. And when at the time of the division there are present the relatives, and the orphans and the poor, then feed them from the property and speak to them a fair speech. And let people who, if they had to leave weak offspring behind them, would be afraid on their own account, be afraid now on other people's account; then let them reverence God, and speak an upright speech.

Surely, those who swallow the property of the orphans unjustly, swallow nothing but fire into their bellies, and they shall soon enter into the flaming fire.

God commands you respecting your children: for the male a share equal to that of two females; then if they be all females, more than two, so for them is two-thirds of what is left; and if there be only one, for her is one-half: and for each of the deceased's parents is one-sixth of what is left if he or she leave a child; but if the deceased leave no child, and the heirs be his or her parents, then for the mother is one-third. But if there be brothers of the deceased, then there is one-sixth for the mother — this, after payment of the legacies bequeathed or debts. You have your fathers and your sons, you know not which of them is nearer to you in benefit; this is a stated proportion fixed by God; surely God is Knowing, Wise.

And for you is one-half of what is left by your wives, if they have no issue; but if they have issue, then you shall have a fourth of what they leave, after payment of the legacies bequeathed by her or the debts. And for them your wives is one-fourth of what you leave if you have no issue, but if you have issue, then for them is one-eighth of what you leave, after the payment of the legacies bequeathed by you, or the debts. And if the deceased man whose estate is to be inherited leave neither father nor children, or if a deceased woman be in the same condition, and the deceased has a brother or a sister, then for each one of them is one-sixth. Then if they be more than this, they are sharers in the one-third, after payment of the legacies bequeathed or the debts; such legacies and debts not being harmful to others; this is a command from God, and God is Knowing, Gentle.

These be the limits fixed by God; and as to him who obeys God and His messenger, He will cause him to enter the gardens beneath which flow rivers, abiding therein; and this is the great attainment. And as to him who disobeys God and His messenger and transgresses His limits, He will cause him to enter the fire, abiding therein; and for him is a degrading agony.

And should any of your women-folk commit an act of indecency, then call against them four witnesses from amongst yourselves, so that if the evidence is established, then confine them to their houses until death gives them their full reward, or God makes for them a way.

And there may be two males amongst you who commit the same, then inflict some penalty on them both, but if they turn to God and do good, then leave them alone. Surely, God is oft-Returning, Merciful. This promise of turning on God's part is for those who do an evil act through ignorance, then quickly turn to Him; towards such people, therefore, God turns, for He is Knowing, Wise.

But there is no turning in favor of those who go on doing evil until death approach one of them and he should say: — "Surely, now I repent." Nor is this turning for those who die whilst they are unbelievers; for such We have prepared a painful agony.

O ye who believe! It is not lawful for you to inherit women by force; and prevent them not from remarrying in order to take away part of what you have given them, except in case they commit a clear act of indecency; and consort with them with fairness. Then, if you dislike them, it may be that you dislike a thing, whilst God has appointed a great deal of good therein.

And if you should desire to change one wife for another, and you have given one of them a heap, then take not anything thereof. Will you take it unjustly and with open sinfulness? And how can you take it when one of you has gone into the other,

205

and the wives have taken from you a most firm covenant? And marry not those women whom your fathers have married, but what is past is past; surely such marrying is an indecency and a heinous affair; and an evil way.

Forbidden to you are — your mothers, and your daughters, and your sisters, and your paternal aunts, and your maternal aunts, and the daughters of a brother, and the daughters of a sister, and the mothers who have given you suck, and your foster-sisters, and the mothers of your wives, and your step-daughters, who are being brought up under your care, from wives with whom you had intercourse, but if you have not had intercourse with them, then there is no harm for you, and the wives of your sons who are from your own loins, and it is forbidden to you to have two sisters as wives together, but what is past is past; surely God is Forgiving, Merciful.

And forbidden are also married women excepting what your right hand possess — this is God's prescribing for you; and allowed to you are all beyond those mentioned, that you seek them in exchange for what is your own, intending to marry them, not for lust. Therefore as to those with whom you wish to benefit yourselves, give them, then, their stated dowries; and there is no harm on you in what you mutually agree together after the dowry has been fixed. Surely, God is Knowing, Wise.

And he amongst you who has not sufficient means to marry a free believing woman, then he might marry one of those whom your right hands possess from amongst believing maids, and God knows best your faiths, you are all one. Therefore marry them with the permission of their masters, and give them their dowries with fairness, these women being duly brought into marriage not acting for lust, and not being kept as mistresses; so that when they have been brought into marriage, if they then commit an act of indecency, then for them is half of the penalty prescribed for free women. This permission to marry a maid is for him who is afraid of falling into difficulties. And if you wait, it is better for you; and God is Forgiving, Merciful.

O ye who believe! Come not nigh to prayers whilst you are intoxicated until you know what you say, nor when you are polluted — excepting ye be travelers on the road — until you have bathed yourself. But if you be sick, or on journey, or if one of you come from the privy, or in case you have touched women, and if you cannot find water, then take some pure earth and rub your faces and your hands; surely, God is Pardoning, Forgiving.

O ye who believe! Take your precautions, then march forth in separate bodies, or march forth all together. And, indeed, there is one amongst you who tarries behind, then if a happening happens to you he says: — "Indeed God has blessed me, because I was not present with them." And if some good from God be your lot, he would certainly say — not as if there had been any friendship between you and him — "Oh, would that I had been with them, then I would have gained a great gain."

Then let those fight in God's way who sell this world's life for the Future; and as to him who fights in God's way, then should he be killed, or should he conquer, we shall then give him a great reward.

And why should you not fight in God's way? Whilst the weak among men, and women, and children are saying: — "Our Lord! Bring us out of this city whose people are unjust, and make for us a protector from Thee, and make for us a helper from Thee." They who believe, fight in God's way, and they who choose disbelief, fight in the way of the transgressor; then fight ye the friends of the evil-one, surely, the stratagem of the evil-one is weak.

Hast thou not considered those to whom it was said: — "Withhold your hands (i.e. fight not) and keep up the prayer and pay the stated alms." But when fighting has been prescribed for them, a party of them begin to fear men like fearing God, or a stronger fear; and they say: — "Our Lord! Why hast

Thou prescribed fighting for us? Why not let us live for a short term?" Say: "The enjoyment of this world is short, but the Future is better for him who practices reverence"; and you shall not be wronged a bit.

208 Death will claim you, wherever you be, and though you be in strong forts; and if good befall them they say: — "This is from God." And if evil befall them they say: "This is from thee, Mohammed." Say: "All is from God." But what is the matter with this people, they scarcely understand a single matter?

What befalls them of good is then from God? And what befalls them of evil is then from thee? and We have sent thee a messenger to all mankind! But God is a sufficient Witness. He who obeys the messenger, then, surely, he has obeyed God; and he who turns back, then We have not sent thee a guardian over such.

Fight thou then in God's way, thou art not burdened except with regard to thyself; but urge the faithful onward; soon will God withhold the fierceness of those who have chosen disbelief, and God is stronger in respect of force, and stronger in respect of making an example.

He who takes part in doing good has a share therein, and he who takes part in doing evil has a burden therein; and God controls the distribution of all things.

And when you are greeted with a good greeting, then greet with a better greeting, or return the same; surely God is Accountant over all things. God is, there is no deity but He; He will most certainly gather you towards the day of the Awakening, there is no doubt therein. And who is more truthful in news than God?

What is the matter with you, then, that you are divided into two groups with regard to the hypocrites? And God has rejected them for what they did. Do you desire to guide him whom God has caused to be lost? And he whom God causes to be lost, thou shalt not find a way for him.

They wish that you should disbelieve as they have disbelieved, so that you may all become equals, then take not any of them as

friends until they leave their homes in God's way; but if they turn back, then capture them, and shed their blood wherever you find them, and take not any of them as friends or helpers.

Excepting those who join a people betwixt whom and you is a covenant, or those who come to you, their hearts being straitened against fighting you or fighting their own people. And had God wished He might have strengthened them against you so that they would have fought you — so that if they leave you alone, and fight not against you but offer you peace, then God gives you no ground against them.

You will also find others who desire to be safe from you and safe from their people; but whenever they are called back towards corruption, they fall headlong into it: then if they leave you not alone, and offer not peace to you and withhold not their hands, then seize them and shed their blood wherever you find them: and these are the people against whom God has given you a clear authority.

And it is not befitting one believer to kill another, except what happens by mistake; and he who kills a believer by mistake has, therefore, to free a believing person, and the submission of the blood-money to his or her people, unless they remit it as charity. But if the deceased be from a people at enmity with you, he being a believer, then there is still the freeing of a believing person. And if he be from a people betwixt whom and you is a covenant then there is the submission of the blood-money to his people and the freeing of a believing person; but he who finds not the means or the person to be freed then he has to fast two consecutive months; this is a forgiveness from God. And God is Knowing, Wise.

And he who kills a believer intending to do so, his recompense, then, is hell, abiding therein, and God's wrath is upon him and His disapproval, and He has prepared for him a great agony.

O ye who believe! When you set forth in God's way, then clarify, and say not to one who offers you "Peace" — "Thou art not

a believer." Do you seek the wealth of this world? But with God are treasures immense. Such were you, ere this, but God obliged you, hence clarify. Surely, God is aware of what you do.

212

Equal are not those believers who sit down at home having no injury, and those who struggle in God's way with their lives and their belongings. God gives eminence to the strugglers with their lives and belongings in rank over those who sit down; and God promises good to all; and God gives eminence to the "strugglers" over the "sitters" by a great reward: Great ranks from Him and forgiveness, and mercy. For God is Forgiving, Merciful.

Surely, there are those whom the messenger-spirits shall give their full reward whilst they are unjust to themselves. They shall say: — "What state were you in?" They shall answer: — "We were weak in the earth." They will say: — "Was not God's earth vast, so that you could emigrate therein?" Then these are the people whose abode is hell, and an evil returning-place is that: excepting the weak amongst men, and women, and children, who are helpless and who know not any way. Therefore, as to those, there is hope that God will pardon them; for God is Pardoning, Forgiving.

And he who emigrates in God's way will find in the earth rest-ing-places many, and abundance; and he who sets out from his home, emigrating towards God and His messenger, then death overtakes him, has his reward, surely, settled with God: for God is Forgiving, Merciful. [iv, s]

[THE FOOD]

O YE who believe! Fulfill your engagements. Allowed to you is the eating of the beasts of pasture except those which are nar-rated to you, and forbidden to you is hunting whilst you are in a state of pilgrimage; surely, God commands what He intends.

O ye who believe! Violate not the tokens of God, nor the sacred month, nor the offerings forwarded to Mecca, nor their neck ornaments, nor those who repair to the Sacred House seeking grace from their Lord and His approval, but when you are free from pilgrimage, then you may hunt. And let not the enmity of a people who have prevented you from going to the sacred mosque cause you to transgress against them. And co-operate in doing good and in being reverent, and co-operate not in sin and transgression; and reverence God, surely God is severe in respect of the consequences.

Forbidden to you is the eating of the dead, and the blood, and the flesh of swine, and whatever has been slaughtered in other than the Name of God, and what has been strangled, or stunned to death, or killed by falling, or gored, or what has been eaten by wild animals except what you have purified by slaughtering in the regular way, and what has been sacrificed to the idols, or that you divide it by means of drawing arrows; all this is impious. This day, the unbelievers have despaired of your religion, then fear them not, but fear Me. This day, have I perfected for you your faith, and completed My blessing upon you, and have accepted for you Al-Islam as a religion; but, whoever is forced by hunger without any inclination towards sin, surely, in that case, God is Forgiving, Merciful.

They ask thee as to what is allowed to them. Say: "Allowed to you are the good things, and with regard to the beasts and birds of prey whom you have taught to hunt — by teaching them what God has taught you — then eat out of what they catch for you, and mention the name of God over it, and reverence God, surely God is quick to count."

This day the good things have been made lawful for you; and the food of those who have been given the Book is lawful for you, and your food is lawful for them; and lawful to you are chaste women from among the believers and chaste women from amongst those whom the Book has been given before you, when you have paid them their portions, living chastely,

213

without fornication and without taking them as mistresses; and whoever denies this faith he, then, has nullified his work, and he shall in the Future be a loser.

O ye who believe! When you rise for your prayers then wash your faces, and your arms up to the elbows, and rub your heads, and wash your feet up to the ankles; and if you have become polluted, then purify yourself by a bath; but if you be sick, or on a journey, or if one of you comes from the privy, or if you have touched women and cannot find water to bathe, then take clean earth, rub your faces and your hands therewith; God intends not to cause you any trouble, but He intends to purify you, and to complete His blessing upon you that you may be thankful. And remember the blessing of Allah upon you, and the covenant He has bound you with, when you said: "We hear and we obey," and reverence God.

And God indeed, took the covenant of the children of Israel, and We raised up among them twelve headmen, and God said: "I am with you. If you keep up the prayer, and pay the stated alms, and believe in My messengers, and support them, and send forward to God a goodly sending then I will surely wipe off from you your evils, and I will surely cause you to enter gardens 'neath which flow rivers; whoever, then, of you disbelieves after this, he has thus surely lost the right way."

Then, on account of their breaking their covenant, we deprived them of Our blessing, and We let their hearts become hardened, so that they change the words from their places, and forget a portion of what they were reminded of and thou shalt continue to be told of their treachery therein, except a few of them; forgive them, then, and pass them over. Surely God loves the charitable.

And of those who call themselves Christians We also took their covenant, they also forget a portion of what they were reminded of, wherefore We feed them with enmity and hatred amongst themselves to the day of the Awakening. And God will inform them what they used to do.

O ye people of the Book! Surely, Our messenger has come to you to clarify for you, most of what you used to conceal of the Book, and he passes over a good deal. Surely, there has come to you from God a light, and a clear Book. God guides therewith him who follows His approval into the paths of Peace, and He takes them out of the darkness into the light by His Will, and He guides them towards the straight path.

Surely have they disbelieved who say that God, He, is the Messiah, son of Mary. Say: "Who, then, is capable of doing anything against God, if He should intend to destroy the Messiah, son of Mary, and his mother, and those who are on this earth altogether?" And to God belongs the kingdom of the heavens and the earth, and all that there is between the two. He makes what He pleases. And God is capable of doing all He pleases. And say the Jews and the Christians: "We are the sons of God and His beloved ones." Say: "Why, then, does He cause you to suffer for your sins?" Nay, you are human beings amongst those He has made. He forgives whom He pleases, and He causes to suffer whom He pleases." And to God belongs the kingdom of the heavens and the earth, and whatever is between the two, and towards Him is the return.

O ye people of the Book! Surely, our messenger has come to clarify for you, after a pause of messengers, lest you say: "There came not to us a bringer of glad tidings nor a warner," now, indeed, there has come to you a bringer of glad tidings and a warner. And God is capable of doing all He pleases.

Surely, We have sent down the Torah which contains guidance and light. According to it were judged the Jews by the prophets — they being Moslems — and also by the teachers and the learned on account of their being appointed guardians over the Book of God, and they were witnesses thereof. Hence fear ye not mankind, but fear Me and sell not My signs for a mean price; and whoever judges not according to what God has sent down, these, then, be the people who disbelieve.

And we prescribed therein for them — Life for life, and eye for eye, and nose for nose, and ear for ear, and tooth for tooth, and recompense for wounds; then whoever forgoes the recompense it is a sufficient expiation for him; and whoever does not judge according to what God has sent down, then these be the people who do wrong.

And we caused to follow, in their footsteps, Jesus, son of Mary, confirming that which was before of the Torah, and We gave him the Evangel which contains guidance and light, and confirming that which is before it of the Torah, and a guidance and an admonition for the reverent. And let the people of the Evangel judge by what God has sent down therein; and whoever does not judge by what God has sent down, these, then, are the people who are disobedient.

And We have sent down to thee O Mohammed this Book with the truth, confirming that which is before it of the books, and a protector over all, then judge between them according to what God has sent down and follow not their desires to turn away from that which has come to thee of the truth. For each one of you have We appointed a fountainhead and an open way. And if God had pleased, He might have made you one people, but He disciplines you in what He has given you, therefore excel each other in good deeds; to God is the return of you all, he will inform you, then, as to that in which you used to differ. [v, s]

DECEPTION

ALL that is in the heavens, and all that is in the earth, magnifieth God: His is the kingdom, His is the praise, and He is powerful over all things. It is He who hath created you; and one of you is an unbeliever, and another a believer; and God seeth what ye do. He created the heavens and the earth in truth; and He hath fashioned you and made goodly your forms; and to Him is your journeying. He knoweth what is in the heavens and the earth; and He knoweth what ye hide and what ye manifest; and God knoweth well the secrets of the breast.

Hath not the story come to you of those who disbelieved aforetime, and tasted the evil fruit of their doings, and received an aching torment? That was because when their apostles had come to them with manifestations, they said, "Shall mortal men guide us?" And they believed not and turned their backs. But God had no need of them; and God is Self-sufficient and worthy to be praised! The unbelievers pretend that they shall by no means be raised again. Say: Nay, by my Lord, but ye shall be raised; then shall ye certainly be told of what ye have done: and that is easy with God. Believe then in God and His Apostle, and in the light which we have sent down; for God knoweth perfectly what ye do. The day when He shall gather you together for the Day of Assembly, that is the day of Deception. And whoso believeth in God and doeth that which is right, God shall take away his sins, and He will bring him into the gardens beneath which rivers flow, to dwell there evermore: that is the great prize! But those who believe not, but deny our signs — those shall be the inmates of the fire, to dwell therein for ever; and evil is their journey. There happeneth no misfortune but by God's permission; and whoso believeth in God, He guideth his heart; and God knoweth all things.

Obey God, therefore, and obey the Apostle: but if ye turn away, our Apostle is only charged with a plain message: — God, there is no God but He! Then in God let the faithful trust. O ye who believe! verily in your wives and your children ye have an adversary, wherefore beware of them. But if ye relent and pardon and forgive, then verily God too is Forgiving and Merciful. Your wealth and your children are but a snare: but God, with Him is the great reward. Then fear God with all your might, and hear and obey, and give alms

for your own sakes; and whoso is saved from his own covetous-ness, — these it is who prosper. If ye lend God a good loan, He will double it to you, and will forgive you: for God is Grateful, Mild, knowing the secret and the open; the Mighty, the Wise! [lxiv, P]

IRON

ALL that is in the heavens and the earth magnifieth God, and He is the Mighty, the Wise. His is the kingdom of the heavens and the earth, He giveth life and giveth death, and He is powerful over all things. He is the first and the last, the seen and the unseen, and all things doth He know. It is He who created the heavens and the earth in six days, then ascended the Throne; He knoweth what goeth into the earth and what cometh out of it, and what cometh down from the sky and what riseth up into it; and He is with you, wherever ye be; and God seeth what ye do. His is the kingdom of the heavens and the earth, and to God shall all things return. He maketh the night to follow the day, and He maketh the day to follow the night, and He knoweth the secrets of the breast.

Believe in God and His apostle, and give alms of what He hath made you to inherit; for to those of you who believe and give alms shall be a great reward. What aileth you that ye do not believe in God and His Apostle who calleth you to believe in your Lord? He hath already accepted your covenant if ye believe. It is He who hath sent down to His servant manifest signs to lead you from darkness into light: for God is indeed kind and merciful towards you. And what aileth you that ye give not alms in the path of God, when God's is the heritage of the heavens and the earth? Those of you who give before the victory, and fight, shall not be deemed equal, — they are of nobler degree than those who give afterwards and fight. Yet to all hath God promised the beauteous reward; and

God knoweth what ye do. Who is he who will lend God a good loan? — He will double it for him, and his shall be a noble recompense.

The day ye shall see the faithful, men and women, their light running in front and on their right hand — "Glad tidings for you this day! — gardens whereunder rivers flow, to abide therein for ever": that is the great prize! The day when the hypocrites, men and women, will say to those who believe, "Stay for us, that we may kindle our light from yours." It shall be said, "Go back and find a light." And there shall be set up between them a wall, with a gate in it; and inside, within it, shall be Mercy, and outside, in front of it, Torment! They shall cry out, "Were we not with you?" The others shall say, "Yes! but ye fell into temptation, and waited, and doubted, and your desires deceived you, till the behest of God came, — and the archtempter beguiled you from God." And on that day no ransom shall be accepted from you, nor from those who disbelieved — your goal is the Fire, which is your master; and evil is the journey thereto. Hath not the Hour come to those who believe, to humble their hearts to the warning of God and the truth which He hath sent down? and that they may not be like those who received the Scripture aforetime, whose lives were prolonged, but their hearts were hardened, and many of them were disobedient. Know that God quickened the earth after its death: now have we made clear to you the signs, haply ye have wits! Verily the charitable, both men and women, and they who lend God a good loan, it shall be doubled to them, and theirs shall be a noble recompense.

And they who believe in God and His Apostle, these are the truth-tellers and the witnesses before their Lord: they have their reward and their light. And they who disbelieve and deny our signs — these are the inmates of Hell! Know that the life of this world is but a game and pastime and show and boast among you; and multiplying riches and children

is like rain, whose vegetation delighteth the infidels — then they wither away, and thou seest them all yellow, and they become chaff. And in the life to come is grievous torment, or else forgiveness from God and His approval: but the life of this world is naught but a delusive joy. Strive together for forgiveness from your Lord and Paradise, whose width is as the width of heaven and earth, prepared for those who believe in God and in His Apostle. That is the grace of God! who giveth it to whom He pleaseth; and God is the fount of boundless grace. There happeneth no misfortune on the earth or to yourselves, but it is written in the Book before we created it: verily that is easy to God! — that ye may not grieve over what is beyond you, nor exult over what cometh to you; for God loveth not any presumptuous boasters, who are covetous and commend covetousness to me. But whoso turneth away, — verily God is Rich and worthy to be praised.

We sent Our Apostles with manifestations, and We sent down by them the Book and the Balance, that men might stand upright in equity, and We sent down Iron, where is great strength and uses for men, — and that God might know who would help Him and His Apostles in secret: verily God is strong and mighty. And we sent Noah and Abraham, and we gave their seed prophecy in the Scripture: and some of them are guided, but many are disobedient. Then we sent our apostles in their footsteps, and we sent Jesus the Son of Mary, and gave him the Gospel, and put in the hearts of those that follow him kindness and pitifulness; but monkery, they invented it themselves! We prescribed it not to them — save only to seek the approval of God, but they did not observe this with due observance. Yet we gave their reward to those of them that believed, but many of them were transgressors. O ye who believe, fear God and believe in His Apostle; He will give you a double portion of His mercy, and will set you a light to walk by, and will forgive you: for God is forgiving and merciful: — that the People of the Scripture may know that they have not power over aught of God's grace; and that grace is in the hands of God alone, who giveth to whom He pleaseth: and God is the fount of boundless grace. [lvii, P]

[THE REPENTANCE]

THIS is a riddance proclaimed by God and His messenger in respect of those pagans with whom you Moslems had made a covenant. Then walk ye in the land for four months from date and know that you cannot escape God, and that God will put the disbelievers to shame. And this is a proclamation from God and His messenger to men on the day of the great pilgrimage that God is rid of the pagans — and so is His messenger. If you then turn towards Him it is then better for you. But if you turn back, then know that you cannot escape God. And give thou tidings of a painful agony to those who disbelieve.

But as to those pagans with whom you made a covenant, then they did not make default towards you in anything and did not help anyone against you; fulfill, then, their covenant in their favor up to their term, surely God loves the reverent. But when the sacred months have elapsed then shed the blood of the pagans wherever you find them, and seize them and besiege them and lie in wait for them at every place of observation. But if they turn to God, and keep up the prayer and pay the stated alms, then let them alone on their path. Surely God is Forgiving, Merciful.

And if anyone of the pagans ask thee for refuge, then give him refuge till He hears God's word, then dispatch him to his place of safety. This is so because surely they are a people who do not know.

How shall there be a covenant in favor of the pagans with God and His messenger? except as to those with whom you cove-

nanted near the sacred mosque, then as long as they keep upright towards you then you should also keep upright towards them, surely God loves those who practice reverence. How can it be? And if they were to be powerful over you they would pay no heed to your ties of relationship or of agreement. They wish to please you with their mouths, and their hearts dissent, and most of them are disobedient. They have bartered God's signs for a mean price, then they keep back from His path. Surely evil are the deeds which these people do. They pay no heed with regard to a believer as to the ties of relationship or of agreement, for they are a people who transgress. But if they turn to God and keep up the prayer, and pay the stated alms, then they are your brethren in faith. And We make plain the signs for a people who know.

And if they break their oaths after covenant made, and scorn you on account of your faith, then fight the ringleaders of the disbelievers; surely oaths are of no use to them; do this: perhaps they will keep back. Why will you not fight a people who have broken their oaths and they resolved to turn out the messenger, and they began the fight the first time? Are you afraid of them? But God has a better right for you to fear Him if ye be believers.

Fight them, God will cause them to suffer at your hands, and He will put them to shame, and He will help you against them, and He will heal the breasts of the people who believe. And He will take away the anger of their hearts. And God will turn towards whom He please. For God is Knowing, Wise. Do you think you will be left alone before God has distinguished those who have struggled from amongst you and who have not taken besides God, and excepting His messenger and excepting the faithful, any secret friend? And God knows what you do.

It is not the business of the pagans to build or to visit God's mosques, bearing witness against themselves of faithlessness. They are a people whose deeds go for nothing. And in the fire they abide. Only he builds or visits God's mosques who believes in God and the Future day, and who keeps up the prayer and gives the stated alms, and fears none except God, therefore these are the people who may hope to be of those who are guided. And do you make the giving of drinking-water to the pilgrims and the building or visiting of the sacred mosque equal to the work of one who believes in God and the Future day, and struggles in God's path? They are not equal in God's sight. And God guides not the people who are unjust.

Those who believe and leave their homes and struggle in God's path with their wealth and their lives have a bigger rank with God. And these are the people who win. Their Lord gives them glad tidings of mercy from Him, and of satisfaction and of gardens in which there is for them a lasting comfort: they abide therein all the time. Surely the reward which is with God is great.

O ye who believe! Take not your fathers and brothers as allies if they love faithlessness more than faith, and he amongst you who allies with them, then he is of the people who are unjust. Say: "If your fathers and your sons and your brethren and your mates, and your relations, and your belongings which you have earned and your trade of whose stoppage you are afraid, and the residences which please you are dearer to you than God and His messenger and the struggling in His path; then wait till God sends His command." For God loves not the disobedient people.

Certainly God has already helped you in many fields, and on the day of Honain when your large numbers made you look strange, but they availed you naught and the land, in spite of its vastness, became straitened to you, then you turned back flying. Then God sent down His calm upon His messenger and upon the faithful, and He sent armies which you saw not, and He made the disbelievers suffer. And this is the reward of the disbelievers. Then God will turn hereafter upon whom He pleases: for God is Forgiving, Merciful.

O ye who believe! The pagans are altogether filthy, then let them not approach the holy mosque after this year of theirs, and if you be afraid of poverty then God will, in time, make you rich out of His grace if He please. Surely God is Knowing, Wise. Fight those who believe not in God nor in the Future day, and who forbid not what God has forbidden, or His messenger, and who believe not in the true faith from amongst those who have been given the Book until they pay the required tax with their own hands, and acknowledge their subjection.

And the Jews say: "Azra is the son of God," whilst the Christians say: "The Messiah is the son of God." These are their sayings with their mouths; they copy the saying of those who disbelieved before them. God's displeasure be upon them! How do they turn away? They have adopted their learned men and their monks as lords besides God, and also the Messiah son of Mary. And they were ordered to worship none but one God; there is no deity but He. Gloried be He, away from what they join. They wish to put out the light of God with their mouths, and God is not going to stop till He has completed His light, averse though the disbelievers be. It is He who has sent His messenger with the guidance and the true faith that He may cause it to be on the top of all faiths, averse though the pagans be.

O ye who believe! The majority of the learned in theology and the monks most surely, wrongfully swallow the wealth of the people, and keep back from God's path. And as to those who hoard gold and silver and spend it not in God's path, give them, then, the tidings of a painful agony: on a day when these things shall be heated in hell-fire, and their foreheads, and their sides, and their backs shall be branded therewith: it will be said: "This is what you hoarded for yourselves, taste then what you did hoard."

Surely the number of months with God is twelve months, so fixed in God's knowledge the day He made the heavens and the earth; of these four are sacred. This is the established faith. Then do no wrong in these months to yourselves, and fight all the pagans as they fight you all. And know that God is with those who practice reverence.

The postponement of a sacred month is an addition of the days of disbelief, those who choose disbelief are misguided thereby: they declare it non-sacred one year and sacred another year in order to make up the number of the sacred months fixed by God, so that they make non-sacred what God has made sacred. Fair-seeming to them are their evil deeds: And God guides not the unbelieving people.

O ye who believe! What reason have you, when you are asked to set forth in God's path, to sit down heavy in the land? Are you better satisfied with the life of this world than the Future? But the enjoyment of the life of this world compared with that of the Future is nothing but little. If you set not forth, He will cause you to suffer a painful suffering, and He will exchange for you another people, and you will do Him no harm. For God is capable of doing all He pleases.

O thou prophet! Strive against the disbelievers and the hypocrites, and be strict against them; and their abode is hell; and an evil place is that to go back to.

They will swear by God that they did not say it; and most surely they have spoken the word of disbelief and have disbelieved after their Islam, and they made up their minds to gain something which they did not; and they were not incensed except because God has enriched them — and so has His messenger — out of His grace; then if they turn to God it will be better for them; but if they turn back, God will cause them to suffer a painful suffering in this world and the Future; and for them there is on this earth no ally and no helper.

And of them are those who covenanted with God, "Surely if He gives us out of His grace we will surely give charity and we will surely be of those who do good." But when He gave them out of His grace they became niggardly of it and turned back whilst they were heedless. Therefore, as a consequence of

their action, He has put hypocrisy in their hearts to the day they shall meet Him, on account of their having acted against God in what they had promised Him and on account of their having been liars. Do they not know that God knows their secrets and their consultations, and that God is the Knower of all things unseen?

There are those who taunt the Moslems who try to win God's love by means of charity, and who taunt those who find nothing to give except their bodily labor, so they scoff at them; God will scoff at them; and for them is a painful agony. Ask forgiveness for them — or ask not forgiveness for them; even if thou ask forgiveness for them seventy times — God will surely not forgive them. This is so because they have disbelieved in God and His messenger; and God guides not the disobedient people.

Those who were left behind were delighted with their sitting down in the absence of the messenger of God, and they were averse to striving with their wealth and their lives in God's path, and they said: "Set ye not forth in this heat." Say: "The fire of hell is stronger in heat." Would that they understood. Then let them laugh little and weep much as a reward for what they did. If then God brings thee back to a party of them so that they should ask thee for permission to set forth, say then: "You shall not set forth with me on any account nor shall you fight together with me against an enemy, surely you were satisfied to sit down the first time, then sit down with those who remain behind." And on no account shalt thou offer prayer for any of their dead nor shalt thou stand by his grave. Surely they disbelieved in God and His messenger and died whilst they were disobedient.

Let not their wealth and their children cause thee to wonder; God only wishes to cause them to suffer on account thereof in this world, and that they may part with their souls whilst they are disbelievers. And when a chapter is sent down saying: "Believe in God and strive together with His messenger," those who have plenty amongst them ask thee for permission to stay away, and they say: "Leave us to remain with those who sit down." They are satisfied to remain with those who are left behind and a seal has been set upon their hearts, so that they understand not. But the messenger and those who believe with him strive with their wealth and their lives, and these are the people who shall have the good things, and these are the people who succeed. God has prepared for them gardens 'neath which flow rivers, they shall abide therein. This is the great triumph. [ix, s]

227

THE VICTORY

VERILY we have won for thee a clear Victory — that God may forgive thee thy former and latter sins, and fulfill His grace to thee, and guide thee on the straight way, and that God may help thee mightily. He it is who sent down peace into the hearts of the faithful, to strengthen their faith with faith, (for God's are the armies of the heavens and the earth, and God is All-knowing and Wise): to bring the faithful, men and women, into gardens beneath which rivers flow, to dwell therein for ever, and to take away their offenses; and that is the great prize with God: and to torment the hypocrites and the idolaters, men and women, who think of God an evil thought; there shall come upon them a turn of evil, and God is wroth with them and hath cursed them, and hath prepared Hell for them, and evil shall be their journey. God's are the armies of the heavens and the earth, and God is Mighty and Wise!
Verily we have sent thee as a witness and a herald of gladness and a warner, that ye may believe in God and in His Apostle; and may revere Him, and honor Him, and magnify Him morning and evening. In truth, they who swear fealty to thee, do but swear fealty to God: the hand of God is upon their hands! Whosoever therefore breaketh it, breaketh it only to

his own hurt; but whosoever is true to what he hath covenanted with God, He will give him a great reward.

The Arabs of the desert who were left behind will say to thee,
"Our property and our families employed us; so ask pardon
for us." They speak with their tongues what is not in their
hearts. Say: But who can obtain aught for you from God, if He
design for you harm, or design for you benefit? Nay, God is acquainted with what ye do! Nay, ye thought that the Apostles
and the faithful would not come back to their families any
more, and that seemed good in your hearts, and ye thought an
evil thought, and ye are a lost people. And whosoever believeth not in God and His Apostle — verily we have made
ready a flame for the unbelievers! And God's is the kingdom
of the heavens and of the earth; He forgiveth whom He will,
and He tormenteth whom He will: and God is Forgiving,
Merciful! They who were left behind will say when ye go
forth to the spoil to take it, "Let us follow you." They would
fain change the Word of God. Say: Ye shall by no means follow us; thus hath God said already. Then they will say, "Nay,
ye are jealous of us." Nay, they are men of but little understanding. Say to those who were left behind of the Arabs of
the desert, Ye shall be called out against a people of mighty
valor; ye shall fight with them, or they shall profess Islam. If,
therefore, ye obey, God will bring you a goodly reward; but
if ye turn your backs as ye turned your backs before, He will
torment you with aching torment. For the blind it is no crime,
and for the lame no crime, and for the sick no crime to turn
the back. And whoso obeyeth God and His Apostle He shall
bring him into gardens whereunder rivers flow: but whoso
turneth his back, He will torment him with aching torment.
Well-pleased was God with the believers, when they sware fealty
to thee under the tree; and He knew what was in their hearts:
therefore did He send down tranquility upon them, and rewarded them with a victory near at hand, and many spoils to
take, for God is Mighty and Wise! God promised you many

spoils to take, and sped this for you; (and He held back men's hands from you, that it might be a sign to the faithful, and that He might guide you on the straight way); and other spoils which ye could not take: but now hath God compassed it, for God is powerful over all. If the unbelievers had fought against you, they would assuredly have turned their backs; then would they have met with no protectors or helper. This is God's way which prevailed before: and no changing wilt thou find in God's way. And He it was who held back their hands from you, and your hands from them, in the valley of Mecca, after that He had given you the victory over them; for God ever seeth what ye do. These are they who believed not, and kept you away from the Sacred Mosque, as well as the offering, which was prevented from reaching its destination. And but for the faithful men and women, whom ye did not know and might have trampled, so that guilt might have lighted on you on their account without your knowledge, that God might bring whom He pleased into His mercy; had they been separate, we had surely punished the unbelievers among them with a grievous torment. When the unbelievers had put disdain in their hearts, — the disdain of ignorance, — God sent down His tranquility on His Apostle and the faithful, and fixed firmly in them the word of piety, for they were most worthy and fit for it, and God well knoweth all things. Now hath God spoken truth to His Apostle in the night vision: "Ye shall surely enter the Sacred Mosque, if God please, safe, with shaven heads, or hair cut; ye shall not fear, for He knoweth what ye do not know; and He hath ordained you, besides that, a victory near at hand." It is He who hath sent his Apostle with the guidance and the religion of truth, to make it triumph over every religion; and God is witness enough!

Mohammed is the Apostle of God, and those of his party are vehement against the infidels, but compassionate to one another. Thou mayest see them bowing down, worshiping,

seeking grace from God, and His approval; their tokens are on their faces — the traces of their prostrations. This is their likeness in the Torah, and their likeness in the Gospel, like a seed which putteth forth its stalk, and strengtheneth it, and it groweth stout, and standeth up upon its stem, rejoicing the sowers — to anger unbelievers thereby. To those among them who believe, and do the things that are right, God hath promised forgiveness and a mighty reward.   [xlviii, P]

HELP

WHEN the Help of God and victory come, and thou seest the people entering the religion of God in troops; then magnify the praises of thy Lord, and seek forgiveness of Him; verily He is ever relenting.   [CX, P]